NORTH KOREA INVADES THE SOUTH

ACROSS THE 38TH PARALLEL
JUNE 1950

GERRY VAN TONDER

Pen & Sword
MILITARY

To my wife Tracey

First published in Great Britain in 2018 by
PEN AND SWORD MILITARY
an imprint of
Pen and Sword Books Ltd
47 Church Street
Barnsley
South Yorkshire S70 2AS

Copyright © Gerry van Tonder, 2018

ISBN 978 1 52670 818 2

The right of Gerry van Tonder to be identified as the author of this work
has been asserted in accordance with the Copyright, Designs and Patents Act 1988.

Typeset by Aura Technology and Software Services, India
Maps, drawings and militaria in the colour section by Colonel Dudley Wall
Printed and bound by CPI Group (UK) Ltd, Croydon, CR0 4YY

Pen & Sword Books Ltd incorporates the imprints of Pen & Sword
Archaeology, Atlas, Aviation, Battleground, Discovery, Family History, History, Maritime, Military,
Naval, Politics, Railways, Select, Social History, Transport, True Crime, Claymore Press, Frontline
Books, Leo Cooper, Praetorian Press, Remember When, Seaforth Publishing and Wharncliffe.

For a complete list of Pen and Sword titles please contact
Pen and Sword Books Limited
47 Church Street, Barnsley, South Yorkshire, S70 2AS, England
email: enquiries@pen-and-sword.co.uk
website: www.pen-and-sword.co.uk

CONTENTS

The Task Force Smith memorial, Osan City, South Korea. (Photo Captain Jonathon Daniell)

TIMELINE

1880s

After invading Korea in 1875, Japanese commercial and mining concerns move into Korea in large numbers.

1882

Korea and the US sign an entente cordiale agreement

1894–95

Japan and China resort to conflict to determine ownership of Korea. China is defeated.

1904

February: The Russo-Japanese War breaks out, as the two competing imperial powers in the region fight over southern Manchuria and Korea.

1905

September: After a conclusive Japanese naval victory at the Battle of Tsushima in May 1905, in which two-thirds of the Russian fleet is destroyed, the American-mediated Treaty of Portsmouth ends hostilities. Russia agrees to withdraw from Manchuria and acknowledges that Korea falls under the Japanese sphere of influence.

November: Japanese troops take Seoul, shooting Korean Prime Minister Han Kyu-sŏl who refuses to hand over power to Japan. Japan gives Korea protectorate status.

1908

November: The Root-Takahira Agreement is signed between the US and Japan, officially recognizing their respective territorial rights in the region. In accepting the US annexation of the Kingdom of Hawaii and the Philippines, the implication is that Japan is free to annexe Korea. Both powers acknowledge Chinese sovereignty.

1910

August: Japan formally annexes Korea. Emperor Sunjong of the Yi dynasty relinquishes his authority to Japan.

1918

December: Koreans resident in the US lobby President Woodrow Wilson to support their desire for an independent Korea.

1919
March–April: Korean activists, calling themselves the 1st March, or Samil, Movement, read out the Korean Declaration of Independence in Seoul, sparking the first major resistance to the Japanese occupiers. In nationwide protests, elements of the Japanese police and military massacre more than 7,500 Koreans, while arresting a further 46,000.

1925
18 April: The Communist Party of Korea, led by Kim Yŏng-bom and Pak Hŏn-yŏng, is secretly formed in Seoul.

1929
November: Over four months, anti-Japanese student demonstrations, started in Gwangju, spread throughout Korea.

1931
19 September: After a fabricated act of sabotage on a railway line near Mukden, Japanese forces invade Manchuria (Manchukuo).

1938
December: Japan declares the Greater East Asia Co-Prosperity Sphere concept of a Western-free East Asia, paving the way for its own expansionist designs.

SEOUL BOMB OUTRAGE

Narrow Escape of Korea's New Governor
Shanghai, Saturday
Seoul advices state that a bomb has been thrown at Baron Saito [Japanese Viscount Saitō Makoto], who escaped unhurt.

Reuter's Agency learns that the attempt at assassination was made just as his Excellency was driving away from the station in a carriage last Wednesday. The bomb exploded with great violence, and twenty-nine spectators were injured, but although the carriage was penetrated in three places by splinters, Baron Saito was uninjured. The assailant has not yet been identified.

There is much seething unrest in Korea. The Koreans are intense lovers of freedom, and do not accept Japanese domination. In 1910, Korea was, by treaty, annexed by their neighbour, which has since followed the policy of Japanising the state in spite of great opposition.

Western Times, Tuesday, 9 September 1919

1940

Early in the year, the Imperial Japanese Army seizes Longzhou on the Chinese–Indochina border to close the rail route from Hanoi.

5 September: Amphibious Japanese forces move into Indochina.

22 September: Vichy France capitulates to the Japanese and allows them to station troops in French Indochina.

1941

July: Japan places long-range bombers on southern Indochina.

7 December: Japan attacks Pearl Harbor.

1945

February: At Yalta, the western Allies and the Soviet Union agree to a post-war trustee-ship of Korea.

July: The North Korean Democratic People's Front and the North Korean Labour Party are formed. The US army prepares for deployment to Korea.

The USS *Shaw* (DD-373) at Pearl Harbor as Japanese bombs detonate her forward magazine. (Photo US Navy)

6 August: The world's first atomic bomb used in anger is dropped by the US over Hiroshima, Japan.

8 August: The Soviets join the Allies in the war against Japan.

9 August: US President Harry S. Truman authorizes a second atomic bomb on Japan, this time over Nagasaki. Russian troops invade Manchuria.

15 August: Japan surrenders and President Truman signs the instrument allowing for the temporary divide of the Korean peninsula at the 38th Parallel: Soviet forces to the north and American forces the south.

December: The Allies agree to the setting up of a joint US-Soviet commission to facilitate a process that will culminate in Korean independence.

1946

February: Kim Il-sung, who had spent the latter half of the war training with Soviet troops, is appointed at the head of a Marxist-Leninist provisional government in the Soviet zone: the People's Committee of North Korea.

May: The US and USSR fail to agree on a future unified Korea.

1947

May: A second US–USSR meeting to discuss Korea's future also ends in deadlock.

September: The US takes the Korean question to the United Nations.

November: Despite Soviet opposition, the UN accepts a US-endorsed plan for global elections in Korea to vote for a single government.

Soviet Red Army troops in North Korea, October 1945. (Photo US Army)

1948

North Korea refuses to allow the United Nations Temporary Commission on Korea (UNTCOK) across the 'border'.

February: UNTCOK declares that elections should go ahead in all areas that allowed the commission access. The Korean People's Army is formalized. The American Joint Chiefs of Staff urge the withdrawal of US forces from Korea.

April: US President Truman accepts National Security Council's (NSC) paper No. 8 as the basis for America's foreign policy on Korea: assist with military training and the Korean economy only, and not with its defence.

Guerrillas of the South Korean Labour party (SKLP), a communist group opposed to a separate South Korea, attack the police on Cheju-do Island, south of the tip of the Korean peninsula. The South Korean government reacts violently, and an estimated 14–30,000 men, women and children die.

10 May: Elections are held, but only in South Korea.

June: South Korea forms a national assembly.

July: The North Korean People's Congress draws up its own constitution. Syngman Rhee is elected the first president of South Korea.

August: South Korea formally becomes the Republic of Korea (ROK).

Elections in North Korea result in the formation of the Supreme People's Assembly.

September: Moscow withdraws its troops from North Korea.

American and Soviet troops meet in Korea, 1945. (Photo Don O'Brien)

The Democratic People's Republic of Korea (DPRK) is proclaimed, with Kim Il-sung as the first North Korean leader.

October: The Soviet Union recognizes the DPRK.

The SKLP foments an anti-Rhee government rebellion of ROK troops at the port of Yŏsu, which spreads to inland towns. Government kill up to 2,000 as they suppress the uprising.

December: The UN declares that the ROK is the only legitimate Korean government.

1949

June: The last US combat forces leave South Korea.

July: The US Korea Military Advisory Group (KMAG) starts its work.

October: With the communist victory over nationalist forces, Mao Zedong proclaims the People's Republic of China (PRC)

1950

February: The USSR and PRC conclude an agreement on friendship and alliance.

March: After investigating rumours of an impending North Korean invasion of the south, US military intelligence finds that it is not imminent.

May: The majority of members elected to the ROK national assembly are against the Syngman Rhee regime.

OUR FUTURE RELATIONS WITH CHINA

By an Old China Hand

The empty shell of government in Nanking has fallen to the Communists; the rump of the Nationalist Government has retreated to Canton, where it will have no more than a nuisance value; the Communists are the *de facto* Government of China, and the world waits anxiously to see what they will do with her.

Let there be no mistake. The core of the Communist movement is Marxist through and through. Outside there is a large following of young people who have flocked to the Red Flag (as years ago their predecessors flocked to the Kuomintang) more from eagerness to do something for China and disgust with the Nationalists than from any clear political conviction. But the heart of the movement is Moscow-inspired, and many of its members are Moscow-trained.

Yet somehow the notion of a Chinese Kremlin does not seem to fit. Communism has never yet been tested as a national Government in any country like China. The Russians have an inherited serf-like mind; it is easy for Stalin to impose his will on them.

Yorkshire Post and Leeds Intelligencer, Tuesday, 26 April 1949

June: Following an abortive attempt by the Democratic Front to lobby for fresh general elections that will include both Koreas, the DPRK makes public its plans for a unified Korea.

25 June: Massed North Korean troops, armour and artillery cross the 38th Parallel, invading South Korea.

26 June: The evacuation of US nationals from Seoul commences.

27 June: The US Far East Air Force (FEAF) is deployed to provide air cover for the evacuation from Seoul to the port of Inch'ŏn.

The UN comes out against the invasion, calling it a breach of peace.

The US Seventh Fleet moves into station in the Formosa Straits.

28 June: The Korean People's Army (KPA) takes Seoul.

29 June: The US commences the bombing of certain targets in the DPRK.

30 June: US President Truman consents to the deployment of ground troops in Korea, and orders a mobilization of reserves.

1 July: Elements of the US 24th Infantry Division – Task Force Smith – arrive in Korea.

Task Force Smith, the first US ground forces in South Korea, arrive by train in South Korea. (Photo US NARA)

3 July: US and British carrier-borne fighter aircraft attack DPRK airfields.

5 July: Task Force Smith sustains heavy losses as it withdraws from Osan.

8 July: Upon being asked by the UN to assume control of its peace efforts in Korea, Truman appoints General Douglas MacArthur to head United Nations Command (UNC) forces.

10 July: The US 25th Infantry Division starts to arrive in Korea from Japan.

12 July: Lieutenant General Walton H. Walker is placed in command of UNC ground troops.

18 July: US 1st Cavalry Division starts to arrive in Korea.

20 July: The KPA takes Taejŏn as the US 24th and 25th infantry divisions counterattack at Okch'ŏn to stall the KPA while defences are strengthened along the Naktong River.

29 July: The first of the US 2nd Infantry Division starts to arrive in Korea.

1 August: Yakov Malik, Soviet delegate to the UN, takes over as president of the UN Security Council.

2 August: The US 1st Provisional Marine Brigade arrives in Korea.

US I Corps mobilized at Fort Bragg in readiness for deployment to Korea.

4 August: UNC forces dig in along the Naktong River, in what becomes known as the Pusan Perimeter.

15 August: The US Eighth Army starts to recruit South Koreans, known as Korean Augmentation to the US Army (KATUSA).

The story of the Korean War. (Photo Divided Families Foundation)

DRAMATIS PERSONAE

Democratic People's Republic of Korea (DPRK – North Korea)
President Kim Il-sung (1912–94)

Born Kim Sung-ju in Japanese Korea, he went to Manchuria with his parents at the age of 14. While attending a Chinese high school in Kirin, both his parents died. According to a September 1949 CIA report on him, Kim fled to Lung-Ching after killing a classmate whose money he had stolen. After later killing a man named Choi, also for money, Kim went to eastern Manchuria, where he came under the influence of notorious Chinese Communist, Li Li-san.

BACKGROUND INFORMATION ON KIM IL-SŎNG

In his residence, the domestic staff included twenty servants, of whom five were cooks. Kim's relations with the staff were very good, and he would occasionally step into the kitchen to discuss the method of cooking some dish or to demonstrate it, for cooking was his hobby. His conversation with the staff was limited to this subject.

Kim preferred all kinds of meats to other foods and ate fish and vegetables only rarely. A basic item of each meal was rice mixed with Indian millet. His favorite food, however, was dogmeat stuffed with chicken, which he demanded every day at both the morning and the evening meals. [Accompanying footnote: 'There is a popular belief in Korea that dogmeat maintains virility'.]

Between 1947 and October 1950, Kim's health was excellent. He worked at his office every day of the week and never missed a day during that three-year period. He smoked moderately and drank little, preferring wine. He regularly retired at 2200 hours and rose at 0400 hours.

Kim played tennis enthusiastically and excelled in the sport and also often went horseback riding. Occasionally he would split wood for exercise. He was an excellent pistol shot and practiced as frequently as time would allow. He did not know how to drive a car. He preferred Russian folk dances of all types to other forms of dancing but from time to time would join in western-style social dancing with his wife or guests at official functions. He entertained high-ranking Soviet and Chinese Communist officials from the embassies frequently.

Central Intelligence Agency Information Report, 17 May 1951

At the age of 18, Kim became a member of the Chinese Communist Youth Group. His ability to execute 'drastic measures' saw him accepted into the Chinese Communist Party (CCP).

In 1919, there had in fact been a General Kim Il-sung, a graduate of the Japanese Military Academy who had been fighting the Japanese in the Paektu Mountains, A brilliant strategist, the general suddenly disappeared, and in October 1931, mentor Li Li-san changed Kim's name to Kim Il-sung and gave him command of a guerrilla unit. Kim started to operate in the same region as his hapless namesake, initiating a campaign against those refusing to adopt the communist ideology. He referred to his mission as 'a fight for the labouring masses'.

Kim was 'brutal and inhuman' in his activities, which was rewarded by being made commander of the Chinese Communist Forces' Second Army. In 1942, he became a senior official of the CCP.

At this time, Soviet leader Josef Stalin came to hear about Kim Il-sung, and set about grooming him for future leadership in Korea. For three years, until the end of the war, future Soviet ambassador to Pyongyang, Terentil Shtykov, personally trained Kim in the practice of communism. Following the surrender of Japan, Stalin appointed Kim secretary-general of the North Korea Communist Party, and from there, the designated head of the North Korean regime. Stalin insisted that Kim retain his adopted name, so that the communists of North Korea would accept him as the famous patriotic general who had bravely fought the Japanese.

Lieutenant General Nam Il (KPA) (1915–76)

Born in Kyŏngwŏn County, Nam's family fled to the Soviet Union when he was still a child. Graduating as a teacher from the Tashkent University, he elected instead to enrol

at the Smolensk Military School. Nam served as an officer in the Red Army during the Second World War. He returned to North Korea in 1946, when he was appointed vice-minister of education for the North Korean People's Committee, then for the DPRK. Several months later, he was made chief of staff at the General Headquarters of Guerrilla Forces, Korean People's Army. Nam assisted the defence ministry with the planning of the invasion of South Korea.

Lieutenant General Nam Il, KPA, sitting in a Soviet-made jeep. (Photo US National Archives)

People's Republic of China (PRC – Communist China)
Chairman Mao Zedong (1893–76)
Born in Hunan Province, Mao was a founder member of the Chinese Communist Party in 1921. Dedicating his life to his well-known communist ideology, after a protracted struggle against Nationalist Chinese forces, on 1 October 1949, the victorious Mao proclaimed the People's Republic of China (PRC). The Chairman's means of perpetuating his revolution were ruthless, constructed on the foundation of the death and imprisonment of millions: 'A revolution is not the same thing as inviting people to dinner or writing an essay or painting a picture or embroidering a flower.' Mao was particularly concerned about developments in the Korean peninsula. His neighbour, at all costs, and by his definition, would have to be 'friendly'.

Republic of Korea (ROK – South Korea)
President Syngman Rhee (1875–1965)
Born in Hwanghae Province, Korea, Rhee was schooled in both Confucianism and at an American Methodist missionary school. His turn-of-the-century anti-Japanese activities saw him incarcerated by the Japanese, during which Rhee adopted Christianity. After his

Lieutenant General Walton H. Walker and Brigadier General John H. Church greet Chief of Staff General J. Lawton Collins. (Photo US Army)

release in 1904, he went to the US where he studied at Harvard and George Washington universities. With a PhD from Princeton, Rhee returned home in 1910, at the time that Imperial Japan had established a solid grip over the whole peninsula. Consequently, Rhee went into exile in the US for thirty-five years, and became president of the Korean Provisional Government. A zealous advocate of Korean independence, upon his return to Korea in October 1945, Rhee quickly alienated himself from the Americans with his overt vociferous anti-Russian rhetoric. While Kim Il-sung successfully set up the North Korean organs of government in early 1947, factionalism was rife in the south. Assassinations characterized the political scene, but, and despite difficult relations with Washington, the US chose Rhee as their candidate to head a South Korean government. Elections in May 1948 brought conservatives to power and the new national assembly voted overwhelmingly for Rhee to become the first president of the newly established Republic of Korea (ROK). Unification of Korea would remain at the top of Rhee's political agenda.

Ambassador to US John Myŏn Chang (1899–1966)
Born in Inch'ŏn, Chang was schooled in Seoul at a Christian institution, before attending a Catholic arts college in the US. By now a staunch Catholic, on his return to Korea Chang took up lay preaching and teaching. Despite only entering mainstream politics in 1946, within two years he had been elected on to the Constitutional Assembly. In 1948, he was a delegate to the third UN conference in Paris, at which the UN recognized South Korea as the only legitimate government on the peninsula. The following year, Chang became the first Korean ambassador to Washington.

United Kingdom
Prime Minister Clement R. Attlee (1883–1967)
As British prime minister from 1945 to 1951, the Oxford-educated Atlee was a major player in the determination of British foreign policy toward post-war Korea. He had also been instrumental in the formation of the North Atlantic Treaty Organization (NATO) in 1949. London and Washington, however, and at a time when both powers were focused on the tenuous situation with the Russians in Germany, had divergent policies over Asian politics. For Britain, Hong Kong was of significant importance to a shrinking empire, and as a consequence, had afforded the new People's Republic of China immediate recognition. Britain's entry into the Korean War was largely tentative, driven only by a loyalty to her war ally. In July 1950, Atlee went against his military chiefs, and committed British troops to the UN forces.

United Nations (UN)
Secretary General Trygve Halvdan Lie (1896–1968)
Norwegian Trygve Lie was the UN's first secretary-general, serving for two periods from 1946–1953. A passionate supporter of the Israeli independence cause, socialist Lie declared the North Korean invasion to be an act of aggression against the UN itself, accusing the DPRK of being in breach of the UN Charter. To become known as the 'fifty-three cables',

'U.S. IS PUSHING TOWARDS WAR' SAYS GROMYKO

M. Andrei Gromyko, senior Soviet Deputy Foreign Minister, today branded America, the United Nations Security Council, and Mr Trygve Lie as 'enemies of peace.'

In a strongly-worded statement, quoted in a Tass message received in London today, he declared the US was 'gradually pushing the country step by step towards open war.'

Describing as 'illegal' the Security Council's decision of June 27, authorising intervention in Korea, M. Gromyko said the Council was acting 'not as a body invested with the main responsibility for the maintenance of peace, but as an instrument employed by the United States ruling circles with the object of unleashing war.'

He made a personal attack on the United Nations' General-Secretary, Mr Trygve Lie, whom he accused of having 'obligingly assisted in the gross violation of the United Nations' Charter.'

Generalissimo Chiang Kai-shek said yesterday that the United Nations, by its actions against the North Koreans, had strengthened the confidence of Asiatic people in the world organisation.

Leicester Daily Mercury, Tuesday, 4 July 1950

Lie appealed to UN members for material and military assistance to repel the invasion under a UN command.

Assistant Secretary-General Constantin Zinchenko (1909–)
Ukrainian-born Constantin Zinchenko spent the latter years of the Second World War as a counsellor at the Soviet embassy in London. In April 1949, after a period as Soviet secretary-general to the UN, Zinchenko joined the UN Secretariat. As assistant general secretary, during the Korean War he developed a reputation of hosting informal meetings, generally of a social nature, in his largely unsuccessful efforts to influence the various parties to the conflict.

United States of America (US)
President Harry S. Truman (1884–1972)
Thirty-third president of the US, in office from 1945 to 1953, history will remember Harry S. Truman for the finite and cataclysmic manner in which he forced the capitulation of Japan at the end of the Second World War. The American atomic obliteration of the Japanese cities of Hiroshima and Nagasaki was, at the time, the ultimate display of unrivalled military might. In an early Cold War flashpoint, the unflappable Truman scored a

major psychological victory over Stalin's blockade of Berlin in 1949. In Korea, the same two antagonists, Berlin still very fresh in their minds, engaged in a second standoff. This time, however, Truman committed his military might to stop the spread of communism in the region.

Secretary of State Dean Goodersham Acheson (1893–1971)
A graduate of Yale and Harvard, Acheson was US secretary of state from 1949 to 1953, and therefore a key player in the formulation of US foreign policy in the early years of the Cold War. Prior to this appointment, he gained considerable experience in the field while working on the Truman Doctrine and the Marshall Plan. Further to this, he was a significant contributor to the formation of NATO. Against this background, Acheson interpreted the North Korean invasion of the south as a belligerent action by Moscow against the US. Acheson and General MacArthur would agree on very little.

Secretary of Defense Louis A. Johnson
The much-criticized Louis Johnson held office as secretary of defence from March 1949 to September 1950. A lawyer by profession and active Democrat, Johnson was an ardent supporter of Truman's policies of reducing military expenditure and unification of the armed forces – in the case of the latter, he pointed to the success of the Berlin Airlift. In the light of Russia's first atomic test in August 1949, Johnson was fully supportive of Truman's desire to develop the nation's nuclear deterrent capabilities. Military cutbacks of his own making, however, would result in Johnson's demise as secretary of defence. Immediately before the invasion, Johnson had toured the Far East with General Omar Bradley and, on his return to the US two weeks later on 24 June, stated his satisfaction with the disposition of his forces in the region. That night, he was informed that South Korea had been invaded from the north. Over the coming weeks, Johnson would be repeatedly attacked as being directly responsible, through his defence austerity budgets, for the abject failure of US forces to withstand the Red flood from the north.

Senator Joseph R. McCarthy (1908–1957)
Another lawyer, Republican Senator Joseph McCarthy was, at the time, rabidly anti-communist, arguably verging on paranoia. His behaviour of making unqualified and unsubstantiated accusations of communist subversion or incompetence and naiveté – including against Truman, Hoover and Acheson – gave birth to the word 'McCarthyism' to describe his actions. Hysteria took hold in the US when the KPA crossed the 38th Parallel, with a spreading belief that communists held important positions in every aspect of American life.

UN Representative Warren Austin (1877–1962)
Washington's representative to the UN from 1946 to 1953, in the 1930s the lawyer was an active member of a small group of international Republicans who eschewed neutrality, advocating instead increases in military budgets and a much more active foreign policy. As the Cold Water intensified, Austin became stronger in his beliefs in American

6 April 1953

Memorandum for: The Director

Subject: Senator McCarthy

1. Attention is called to an article in the Sunday Star on 5 April regarding Senator McCarthy by Jack Bell, an Associated Press staff writer. This article states:
'Where is Senator McCarthy going next ...?

'Best guess now is that, having taken a whirl at operations of the Voice of America, the State Department's filing system, Government stockpiling, and Greek shipping, his committee will land next on the Central Intelligence Agency.

'That hush-hush organization now is headed by Allen Dulles, brother of the Secretary of State, and formerly was directed by Walter Bedell Smith, undersecretary of State. It probably will feel the force of the McCarthy whirlwind in short order.'

2. It is suggested that consideration be given to discussing with Senator McCarthy the list of names which he presented to us at his hearing so as not to be in a position of seeming to ignore his request, which might lead to more drastic action on his part. This does not include the 'New Leader' material, which is being handled separately and upon which we may have additional time due to the fact that Committee counsel is abroad.

Walter L. Pforzheimer, Legislative Counsel, CIA

internationalism. It came as little surprise therefore, that Austin, seeing himself as a champion of morality, pushed through the UN resolution that promulgated member participation in the armed defence of South Korea under the auspices of the UN.

Ambassador to Seoul John J. Muccio (1900–89)

Italian-born John Muccio, was the first US ambassador to Seoul. As chief of the US mission with economic, administrative and supplies responsibilities, Muccio also directed the Korea Military Advisory Group (KMAG). Shortly before the north's invasion, Muccio had warned the US Congress that the ROK was dangerously underpowered and under-strength, to the extent that it would crumble in the face of a concerted DPRK invasion. However, few paid any attention to his concerns. Six and a half hours after the KPA crossed the 38th Parallel, Muccio informed Washington.

Vice-Admiral Arthur Dewey Struble (1894–1983)

A career naval officer, at the time that the US joined the Second World War, Struble had been executive officer on the battleship USS *Arizona*. His first command was the light cruiser USS *Trenton* in the Pacific. In late 1943, he was appointed chief of staff to Admiral Alan G. Kirk, who was in command of US naval forces during the Allied Normandy invasion in June 1944. Immediately after the Japanese surrender, Struble commanded the Pacific Fleet's mine-clearance operations. Promoted to vice-admiral in 1948, in May 1950, he was given the command of the Seventh Fleet, directing the first carrier-based strikes against Pyongyang when South Korea was invaded. The fleet went on station in the Formosa, or Taiwan, Strait, from where task forces conducted patrols of this disputed stretch of water.

General Douglas MacArthur
Lauded Second World War US army commander and liberator of the Philippines, after receiving the Japanese instruments of peace in Tokyo, General MacArthur assumed command of US occupation forces, including South Korea, as the territory had been a Japanese colony. With the scheduled withdrawal of Soviet and American troops from the peninsula in 1948, Moscow was extremely generous in its supply of military hardware to Pyongyang, but MacArthur did not trust South Korea not to attack the north, so he refused repeated requests from Seoul for war matériel. On 8 July 1950, MacArthur was given command of the US-dominated UN forces in Korea.

General George E. Stratemeyer (1890–1969)
A product of the US Military Academy at West Point, Stratemeyer received his wings in 1917, transferring to the Army Air Corps three years later. In 1936, he was promoted

General Douglas MacArthur greets South Korea's first president, Syngman Rhee. (Photo US Army)

to lieutenant colonel and given command of the 7th Bombardment Group. Promoted to major general in 1942, Stratemeyer went on to direct air operations in the China–Burma–India theatre. From April 1944 to the end of the war in the Far East, he was commander of the US Army Air Force (USAAF), China. Recognized as a skilled tactician with excellent man-management skills, in April 1949 Stratemeyer was posted to Tokyo to assume command of the Far East Air Force (FEAF). This comprised the Fifth Air Force in Japan, the Thirteenth Air Force in the Philippines, and the Twentieth Air Force in Okinawa. Stratemeyer would direct the first aerial attacks against the invading KPA forces as well as the evacuation of Americans from Seoul.

General Joseph Lawton 'Lightning Joe' Collins (1896–1987)

Collins was chief of staff of the US army from 1949 to 1953. Assigned as chief of staff to the Hawaiian Department after the Japanese attack on Pearl Harbor, Collins became a household name after his defeat of the Japanese at Guadalcanal. He was also a veteran of the Normandy landings and the Battle of the Bulge in the Ardennes. Collins was promoted to full general in 1948. He did not believe that Korea was of strategic importance to the US.

Lieutenant General Hoyt S. Vandenberg (1899–1954)

Graduating from West Point in 1923, two years later Vandenberg earned his wings. At the outbreak of war with Japan, he was tasked with supervising the expansion of the Army Air Force. Following a period on General Dwight Eisenhower's staff assisting with the development of plans for North Africa air operations, Vandenberg was appointed chief of staff of the Twelfth Air Force. In August 1944, Eisenhower placed him in command of the Ninth Air Force covering the Allied advance through Europe. In July 1945, now with the rank of lieutenant general, Vandenberg became assistant chief of staff of the USAAF, and succeeded General Spaatz as chief of staff in April 1948. He was a key player in the Berlin Airlift of 1948–49.

General Omar Nelson Bradley (1893–1981)

Commander of the First Army in the June 1944 Normandy landings, Bradley went on the command the 1.3-million-strong Twelfth Army Group in August, the largest ever by a US general. He became the first chairman of the Joint Chiefs of Staff, serving from 1949–53. Promoted to full five-star general the following year, Bradley was a strong advocate of US military intervention in Korea, remaining President Truman's most valuable and trusted military advisor during the conflict.

Lieutenant General Walton Harris Walker (1889–1950)

A veteran of the First World War, during the second global conflict Walker commanded the much-respected XX 'Ghost' Corps, known for its fast pace of advance through Western Europe. In September 1948, Walker was given command of a depleted Eighth Army in Japan, by which time only 10 per cent of the unit's strength had any combat experience.

GENERAL WALKER KILLED IN JEEP CRASH

Lieut.-General Matthew B. Ridgway has been appointed commander of the American 8th Army in succession to Lieut.-General Walton H. Walker who was killed to-day in a jeep accident.

Hundreds of American soldiers saw General Walker killed five miles north of Seoul. He was going north to give a citation to an American unit when he met a southbound convoy on the slippery road.

A Korean lorry driver pulled out of the convoy into the path of the jeep, which braked, skidded and hit the lorry. General Walker was thrown out and run over by the jeep.

General MacArthur issued this statement:' I am profoundly shocked at the death of General Walker. As commander of the United States Army he proved himself a brilliant military leader whom I had just recommended for promotion to the rank of full general.

'His gallantry in actions has been an inspiration to all who have served with him, and his loss will be keenly felt not only by our own country but those allied with us in the defence of freedom on the Korean peninsula.'

It was later disclosed in Tokio that General Walker was on his way to decorate his son, Captain Sam Walker when he was killed.

Nottingham Evening Post, Saturday, 23 December 1950

With the North Korean invasion, in July 1950, and in rapid succession, Walker established his army's forward headquarters in the pivotal town of Taegu, being given operational control of South Korean army units and all UN ground forces. Walker is best known for successfully establishing the Pusan defence perimeter, famously declaring, 'Stand or die … there will be no Dunkirk.'

Major General William B. Kean (1897–1981)

Graduating from the Command and General Staff College in 1939, during the Second World War, Kean was appointed chief of staff of the US 28th Infantry Division, before being promoted to brigadier general and serving under General Omar Bradley in North Africa. Later, as chief of staff of the US First Army, Kean was a key player in the planning of the D-Day Normandy invasion. At the end of the war, and now with the rank of major general, Kean remained with the occupying forces in Germany. He assumed command of the US 25th Division in 1948. Under his command, the division was instrumental in the successful defence of the Pusan Perimeter in late 1950.

Major General William F. Dean (1899–1981)

Slow in moving up the ranks, Dean spent much of the Second World War behind a desk. Only toward the end of the war was he given command of the US 44th Division, for which he was awarded the Distinguished Service Cross. While commanding the US 24th Infantry Division in the early stages of the Korean War, Dean was taken prisoner after the fall of Taejon and a long period lost in the mountains. He was only released after the end of the fighting in 1953.

Major General John Huston Church (1892–1953)

With the US entry into the First World War, Church enlisted and served on the Western Front as a second lieutenant with the US 28th Infantry Regiment. Wounded twice during the war, Church was awarded the Distinguished Service Cross for heroism in action at the Battle of Cantigny. During the Second World War, Church served with the US 45th Division as chief of staff, taking part in the invasion of Sicily, the liberation of Italy, and Operation Dragoon, the Allied invasion of southern France. In the final stages of the war in Europe, Church was promoted to the rank of brigadier general, assistant division commander of the US 84th Infantry Division. He was wounded in action in the Netherlands.

Sent to Korea on a fact-finding mission by General MacArthur at the start of the North Korean invasion, Church became de facto commander of the ground operation in the early stages of the conflict that had caught the Americans completely wrong-footed. Church had strongly recommended to MacArthur that US forces be committed. On 22 July, he assumed command of the US 24th Infantry Division.

Brigadier General William L. Roberts (1891–1968)

Having gone largely unnoticed during the Second World War, Roberts was passed over for promotion to major general, and was due for retirement in 1950. In 1948, he was posted to Korea as an advisor to the US military's Department of Internal Security. After commanding the formation of the Korean Military Advisory Group, KMAG, Roberts was appointed chief at the KMAG's new headquarters in Seoul. Military advisor to Ambassador Muccio, Roberts was tasked with training the South Korean army to a level of combat fitness to be able to withstand an invasion from the north.

Union of Soviet Socialist Republics (USSR)

Premier Josef Stalin (1879–1953)

Born in Georgia, Stalin served as general secretary of the Soviet Communist Party from 1922 until his death in 1953, and premier from 1941. Known for saying he trusted no one, including himself, Stalin had readily agreed to temporary custodianship of Korea north of the 38th Parallel. Unsurprisingly in hindsight, for Stalin this was an ideal opportunity to entrench North Korea in the Soviet sphere of influence – he made certain that North Korea would be a communist state under his personally selected candidate, Kim Il-sung. Already US President Truman's wily adversary in the Berlin crisis, in March and April 1950, Stalin gave the visiting Kim Il-sung his full attention: war matériel and military advisors to assist with his plans for invading the south. Stalin would then step back, urging Red China to take up the reins on behalf of international communism.

UN Representative Andrei Andreyevich Gromyko (1909–1989)

The Soviet Union's foremost diplomat over five decades, as ambassador to the US in 1943, Gromyko was closer to American life and politics than most. From 1946 until taking up the post of ambassador to the UK in 1952, he was the Soviet Union's permanent representative to the UN. In the early days of the body, Gromyko's liberal use of the Soviet veto earned him the sobriquet 'Mr *Nyet*'. A legend in Soviet foreign politics.

Foreign Minister Andrei Ianuarovich Vyshinsky

The vociferous Vyshinsky took over from Molotov as Soviet foreign minister in 1949, serving throughout the Korean crisis until 1953. A close associate of Stalin's, the trained lawyer was the chief state prosecutor during the former's bloody purges of the 1930s. He led the Soviet condemnation of UN involvement in the Korean War, accusing South Korea of starting the war and the US of antagonism in the internal affairs of another nation. For Stalin, Vyshinsky was the ideal instrument to project his deliberate vacillating foreign policies.

Ambassador to Pyongyang Terentil Fomich Shtykov

As Moscow's ambassador in Pyongyang from 1948 to 1951, the highly decorated brigadier general of the Second World War, Shtykov was a key player in the establishment of the North Korean republic, DPRK. An ardent Stalinist, by overseeing staffing selection for the North Korean civil service and being a key participant in the drafting of the fledgling nation's constitution, there can be no doubt that Shtykov had an indelible influence on Korean politics' formative years. An adherent of Kim Il-sung and his policies, it his highly probable that Shtykov influenced Stalin's endorsement of the attack on the south.

UN Delegate Yakov Malik

Career diplomat Malik, served in the Soviet embassy in Tokyo, being appointed ambassador in 1942. He was, however, a Stalin yes-man, to be used as a pawn by the dictator from the time of his appointment as Soviet representative to the UN in 1948. In January 1950, Moscow instructed Malik to walk out of the Security Council in Soviet protest against the refusal to offer a seat on the council to Communist China. In the absence of Malik's right of veto, in what US Secretary of State Acheson described as a 'long helpful Russian boycott', the West had the necessary control of the Security Council to facilitate UN intervention in Korea. Malik was ordered back in August when it was the Soviet Union's alphabetical turn to chair the council, introducing a thirteen-session period of negative leadership and anti-American rhetoric.

INTRODUCTION

THE KOREAN SITUATION

The Soviet-inspired invasion of South Korea and the prompt and vigorous US reaction have overnight changed the complexion of the cold war and will lead to the development of new and critical problems for the US in nearly every quarter of the globe. It is not believed that the USSR desires a global war at this time. It is probable, however, that a concerted attempt will be made to make the US effort in Korea as difficult and costly as possible (The USSR has sizeable forces of Chinese Communist troops at its disposal for this purpose.) The implications to the US of defeat in Korea would be far-reaching. It would become nearly impossible to develop effective anti-Communist resistance in Southeast Asia, and progress toward building a strong Atlantic community would be seriously threatened. A US victory in Korea would also pose serious problems for the US.

Increased demands for the adoption of a vigorous stand by the US against Communist expansion has, in general been favourably received throughout the non-Soviet world. The adoption of this stand, however, implies that any failure by the US to take similarly prompt and effective action to stop any further aggressive moves may have even more serious repercussions to US and Western prestige than would have resulted from failure to come to the aid of South Korea.

The Korean invasion has increased fears that the USSR will take aggressive action in other 'soft spots' on the Soviet periphery, thus tending to create in these areas greater demands for US military and economic aid. The areas most immediately affected are Southeast Asia (particularly Indochina), Iran, Yugoslavia, Greece, and Germany.

Central Intelligence Agency declassified daily report, 30 June 1950

The tripartite Potsdam Conference of July–August 1945 was the final in a litany of meetings at which the 'Big Powers' decided on the complexion of a post-Second World War world. National boundaries were arbitrarily redefined in a give-and-take series of agreements and undertakings that would ostensibly compensate the victors for their losses incurred to rid the globe of Axis expansionism. In reality, the dominating, and largely undeclared motive, was for the United States and the Soviet Union to peg their claims on spheres of influence deemed to be of significant and vital strategic importance.

As the 1940s drew to a close, simmering East–West tensions in Europe inevitably boiled over into confrontation over rights of conquest over Berlin and Germany. Soviet leader Joseph Stalin amassed hundreds of thousands Red Army troops in territories contiguous to eastern Germany, but US President Harry S. Truman was, at the time, head of the only atomic super power, and the first person in the history of mankind to use the atom bomb in anger. In a risky game of strength and diplomatic endurance, sanity prevailed and the Berlin crisis was resolved and a third world war averted.

In the Far East, however, rapidly changing events would see Stalin and Truman again facing up to each other, but this time, the astute Russian would let others do his bidding. The US, as sole occupying force, was in total control of Japan, providing for the establishment of air force and naval bases facing China and the eastern Soviet Union. Chiang Kai-shek had lost the nationalist fight against Mao Zedong, resulting in the birth of the Communist People's Republic of China.

On the Korean Peninsula, by December 1948, Soviet and US forces, by agreement, respectively withdrew from north and south of the 38th Parallel. For the United States, South Korea was of no regional importance, and therefore saw no need to equip the south with military hardware with which to defend itself.

For the north, Stalin's agenda for the peninsula could not have been more different. Moscow selected, groomed, indoctrinated, and trained and equipped Kim Il-sung and his army. Toward the end of the Second World War in the Far East, Soviet armies cleared Chinese Manchuria of the Japanese before handing the territory, on North Korea's border, over to the Chinese Communists. Stalin then sat back, having significantly created a vast swathe of Red to the south of his nation.

With the abject failure of national unifying elections in the divided peninsula and the Democratic People's Republic of Korea of Kim Il-sung snugly under his Red wings, Stalin encouraged the more-than-willing Kim to invade the south. He hoped that the US would then become militarily involved in the defence of the Republic of Korea, which in turn would draw Communist China into the fray – a major test for Washington.

In this the first of six volumes on the Korean War, North Korea launches a massive attack on the south, crossing the 38th Parallel in west-to-east phases. In Washington and Tokyo, the Americans are caught totally by surprise, with most enjoying a leisurely weekend away from the office. Ill-prepared and poorly equipped, South Korean forces and the US troops thrown in to execute holding-only positions suffer humiliating defeat after defeat as the North Koreans sweep down the peninsula in an invasion reminiscent of Hitler's blitzkrieg across a helpless Western Europe.

On 4 July 2017, North Korean leader Kim Jong-un, grandson of Kim Il-sung, test-launched an intercontinental ballistic missile – Hwasong-14 – capable of reaching Alaska. On Friday, 28 July 2017, the North Koreans fired another missile, which travelled 1,000km before landing in the Sea of Japan. Kim Jong-un's ongoing 'testing' of military hardware is in blatant defiance of a United Nations ban, and in spite of international sanctions. Does the rogue nation have a secret agenda to cross the 38th Parallel?

To the reader, the Korean language may seem very alien, particularly when it comes to the names of people and places. In his research, the author came across place names with several spellings, based largely on individual interpretations of Korean phonology. The Korean alphabet, or *Hangul*, has only twenty-one vowel/vowel combinations and nineteen consonants, with pronunciation peculiar to the language. The author has, wherever possible, adhered to accent symbols associated with written words, e.g. the short vowel ŏ.

North Korean propaganda poster depicting the US being driven off by North Korea and her Communist Chinese ally. (Political Art)

1. DIVISIVE SPOILS OF WAR

> Known in the West [in the mid-1800s] as the 'Hermit Kingdom', Korea remained a
> remote and closed peasant society, an undeveloped and relatively mysterious place to
> Americans who knew little of its people, or their culture, language, and history.
>
> *The Korean War and the Central Intelligence Agency*, Dr Clayton Laurie,
> Center for the Study of Intelligence

The US first commenced trading with the Joseon (Chosŏn) kingdom in the 1840s. In the eyes of the West, the label of 'Hermit Kingdom' would remain for decades to come as the players on the booming stage of international economics vied for the potentially lucrative Chinese market and, more latterly, Japan, a nation that was modernizing at a rapid pace while becoming a military power of which to take note.

Following successive victories in two wars with Czarist Russia, in 1905 imperial Japanese troops marched into Korea. Five years later, Japan annexed the whole Korean peninsula, terminating a 500-year-old monarchy and embarking on a 35-year rape of Korea's culture, society and resources. The Japanese masters brutally dealt with even the slightest hint of Korean nationalism, imposing a strict colonial administration suitably armed with secret police and military strength to suppress any form of dissent. In 1919 alone, Japanese troops massacred more than 50,000 Korean participants in independence rallies.

In the early years of Japanese occupation, more than a million Koreans fled the Japanese tyranny, and by 1921, nationalists who were among those who had fled, formed a provisional government in exile. Washington, however, chose to ignore events on the Korean peninsula, turning a deaf ear to repeated pleas from Korean nationalists for right of self-determination facilitated by American intervention.

Even the outbreak of the Second World War, allied with Japanese military expansionism in the Far East, failed to persuade the US to take any notice of Korea. The December 1943 Cairo Declaration, a policy statement arising out of the tripartite summit between US President Franklin D. Roosevelt, British Prime Minister Winston Churchill and leader of Nationalist China Chiang Kai-shek, again showed that Korea was not deemed to be a factor in the ongoing prosecution of the war: after victory over Japan, the declaration 'determined that in due course Korea shall become free and independent'. It was apparently of no consequence not to define 'in due course'. Again, at Yalta in February 1945 and Potsdam in July 1945, Truman, Churchill and Stalin remained ambivalent toward Korea's post-Japanese future.

However, in August, the Soviet Union joined the fray against Japan, now seeing the peninsula as being of 'strategic interest'. Potsdam set the big-power divide at the 38°N line of latitude, a seemingly arbitrary delineation that, to this day, is commonly referred

Su-pei Jih-pao newspaper, Yang-chou, People's Republic of China

16 August 1950

On 8 August 1945, after the US had dropped an atomic bomb on Hiroshima, US newspapers and news agencies made numerous and varied statements about the tremendous power of the atomic bomb. One newspaper stated that one A-bomb is more violent than 30,000 tons of dynamite. Another stated that one A-bomb was equal in force to bombs carried by 2,000 superfortresses. Another said that one A-bomb produces heat equivalent to that produced by the combustion of 5 million pounds of coal. Again, it has been said that all structures within a radius of 50 miles of an A-bomb blast would be damaged. All of these statements are exaggerated and boastful.

A Chinese witness of the Hiroshima bombing was a man by the name of Cheng Chung-chih, of Chin-sha Chen in southern Hopeh. At the time of the bombing, he was confined in a Japanese prison not far from the center of Hiroshima, for having sabotaged some belts on electrical machinery. At first he heard a slight mechanical sound, then, shortly after, the crash and rumble of the explosion. Looking through one of the windows, he saw that the city was on fire. But the prison was not destroyed nor were any of its inmates killed or injured.

On l July 1946, the US carried an A-bomb experiment at Bikini in the Pacific Ocean. Authorities on A-bombs stated in advance that not a living creature near the center of the atomic explosion would be lucky enough to survive. The inhabitants of Bikini were all removed to other islands and a number of pigs and sheep were placed near the scene of the experiment for test purposes. But, when the explosion came, the sheep went right on baaing and munching the grass. Experimental pig No 311 was later examined in a naval laboratory and found to be unharmed and completely normal. The power of an atomic bomb is no more than this.

The warmongers think they can frighten people with the A-bomb; nothing could be more stupid or ridiculous. Furthermore, there is another very important point. No military weapon can be the decisive factor in determining victory or defeat in a war. The decisive factor is the character of the conflict and of the men who wield the weapons. In World War II, was it not Germany who first invented and used magnetic mines? Was it not Germany who invented and used flying missiles and other new types of weapons? But what good were they? We Chinese, from our own experience, understand this truth. In our people's struggle for liberation, did not the reactionary KMT use all kinds of US rifles, guns, tanks, airplanes, and other kinds of superior weapons? But of what use were they? Germany offers a piece of instruction which it would be well for the warmongers to remember. In World War II, German scientists preceded the US in the study of atomic bombs; they constructed in Norway a factory to produce heavy water which was an integral part of

(Continued)

the plant to manufacture A-bombs. But before long, it was destroyed by the Fascist-hating people of Norway.

At present, US warmongers are going contrary to the will of the people of the whole world in using the A-bomb as an instrument for aggression. It is too much to say that the peace-loving war-hating people of the world will not know how to demolish the factory that makes A-bombs. The people of the world are against the use of atomic weapons; the only ones who oppose the prohibition of atomic weapons are the very small number of warmongers. World sentiment in favor of peace is very powerful; the warmongers are a solitary lot. The power of the A-bomb cannot intimidate and restrain people who are struggling for peace. We are confident that the united moral force of the peace-loving people of the world certainly can prevent a new war.

Central Intelligence Agency, information from foreign documents or
radio broadcasts, 7 November 1950

British premier Winston Churchill, US President Franklin D. Roosevelt, and Soviet leader Josef Stalin at the Livadia Palace, Yalta, February 1945. (Photo US NARA)

to as the 38th Parallel. With the capitulation of Japan on 15 August 1945, bringing the Second World War to an end, Soviet and American troops poured into their respective north and south administrative zones to commence the massive exercise of disarming and repatriating 600,000 Japanese military personnel and 70,000 civil servants from Korea. From the decades-long Japanese authoritarian – often barbaric – control, the people of Korea suddenly found themselves politically rudderless, and in a state of indeterminate limbo.

In mid-August, the Red Army occupied the wealthier of the two zones, followed three weeks later by the deployment in the south of the 40,000-strong US XXIV Corps under Major General John R. Hodge. This part of the peninsula had the highest population density, rich agricultural lands, and the country's only major port at Inch'ŏn.

For the average serving American, Korea was far from an attractive posting: 'a miserably poor, primitive, mountainous place with few paved roads or amenities ... jungle hot and steamy in the rainy season ... arctic cold in winter.' Even the war-crippled Japan was considered a better option in which to serve as occupier. The living conditions, language, post-war cutbacks and a territory that held little strategic importance, all contributed to Washington's desire – including Truman and his Joint Chiefs of Staff – to withdraw its whole operation from Korea as expediently as possible.

Then, at a meeting of foreign ministers in Moscow in December 1945, doubt started emerging as to the wisdom of America walking away from Korea. Events in the disputed carving-up of erstwhile Nazi Germany saw cracks starting to appear in Russo-American relations. Moscow's designs to internationalize communism under its wing became increasingly evident. To facilitate this, the Kremlin would spread its ideologies and power by proxy: so-called puppet regimes that would be handsomely rewarded for their loyalty to Moscow.

In China, where the conflict between nationalist and communists had been relegated to the backburner to combat the common Nipponese enemy, a resumption of the bitter war was imminent. In the closing stages of the Second World War, the Soviet Union was able to optimize its war effort in the Far East. In what Moscow referred to as the Manchurian Strategic Offensive Operation, more than 1.5 million Red Army troops, 7,000 artillery pieces, 5,500 tanks and self-propelled guns, 3,700 aircraft and 16,000 Mongolian troops swept into Manchuria, demolishing the depleted 700,000-strong Japanese Kwantung Army, commanded by General Otozō Yamada. More than 500,000 Japanese POWs were sent to Soviet labour camps in Siberia, the Russian Far East and Mongolia.

A significant contributor to the ultimate demise of Japan, the removal of the Japanese in Manchuria and the subsequent withdrawal of the Red Army had far-reaching consequences in the region, particularly for the Koreans. Moscow ignored the plight and pleas of the Chinese nationalists for assistance to capitalize on the void that the sudden departure of the Russians and the Japanese had created in Manchuria. Mao Zedong rapidly expedited the situation, and in doing so, firmly placed everything north of the Yalu River border with North Korea in communist hands.

Imperial Japanese Army 4th Division firing type-92 heavy machine gun, China.

In Korea south of the 38th Parallel, when US administrators arrived with the military in 1945, they encountered political turmoil. The left-wing Korean People's Party (KPR) – quickly banned by US administration – and the pro-American, right-wing movement, the Korean Democratic Party (KDP) were actively vying for political control. In North Korea, however, the Communist Korean Workers' Party under leader Kim Il-sung had a controlling grip on politics, with robust support from his masters in Moscow.

For several months in 1946 and 1947, numerous meetings of an American–Soviet Joint Commission, set up under the remit of the Moscow conference, failed to reach a consensus on Korea's future. The stalemate prompted US Secretary of State George C. Marshall – in the face of Soviet opposition – to take the Korean standoff to the United Nations for the first time. As a first step toward a unified Korea, two months later the UN approved US proposals for democratic elections in Korea. Whilst still desirous to keep Soviet influence out of the peninsula, the US, however, was still disinclined to get involved in anything other than short-term political and military assistance, mainly in an advisory capacity.

In a late development, the Russians and their North Korean allies prevented the newly established UN Temporary Commission on Korea (UNTCOK) from crossing the 38th to assess election logistics in the north. Undeterred, the commission was adamant that the elections would go ahead in the spring. Despite concerns from Australia, Canada, India and Syria, on 10 May elections were held for a 200-seat constituent assembly, questioning the legitimacy of the outcome without the North Korean electorate and the left-wing parties in the south.

In the weeks leading up to the election, there was considerable unrest in the south, notably on Jeju Island off the south coast, where government forces quashed an insurrection fomented by the South Korean Labour Party (SKLP) with unfettered brutality. It is estimated that between 14,000 and 30,000 island inhabitants – 10 per cent – were massacred. Acts of terrorism accounted for a further 600 deaths.

Syngman Rhee's National Association for the Rapid Realization of Korean Independence (NARKKI) won 26 per cent of the vote, taking 55 seats. The Korea Democratic Party (KDP), led by moderate and Rhee supporter, Kim Seong-su, won 29 seats – 14 per cent of votes cast. The largest slice of the ballot – 40 per cent – went to independent candidates, winning 85 seats. It was clear that neither Rhee nor Kim enjoyed any enabling popular support.

A South Korean man voting in Nae Chon, 1948. (Photo US Army)

A Korean national assembly was promulgated in June, and on 18 August 1948, the Republic of Korea (ROK) – South Korea – was born, with Seoul the capital. Later that month, elections in North Korea saw Moscow's henchman, Kim Il-sung, on 9 September become premier of a new communist state: the Democratic People's Republic of Korea (DPRK), its capital P'yŏngyang.

Soviet troops immediately commenced a withdrawal from North Korea, followed by full recognition of the DPRK in October. To the south, and despite the outbreak of insurgent attacks from the north to destabilize South Korea, US National Security Council (NSC) instrument 8 of April 1948, defined US post-election involvement: to assist with the establishment of a self-sufficient economy and armed forces capable of defending the nation on the their own.

In December, the UN declared that the body recognized the ROK as the only legitimate Korean government.

Whilst contending that the ROK would be incapable of repelling an invasion from the north, General MacArthur strongly urged Washington to withdraw its forces from South Korea. On 29 June 1949, the last of the US forces left, leaving behind a few hundred men to establish the Korean Military Assistance and Advisory Group (KMAAG). However, Washington did not leave behind any tanks, anti-tank weapons or aircraft for the new nation. In the DPRK, meanwhile, the Soviet Union supplied Kim Il-sung's Korean People's Army (KPA) with large quantities of armour, artillery, aircraft, and other matériel. Comprehensive Soviet-run training programmes were also introduced.

By early 1950, Truman's Democratic congressmen and the Department of State continued to display a disregard for events in Korea. This apparent blasé attitude drew sharp criticism from the Republicans, especially from senators Robert Taft and Joseph McCarthy.

The so-called period of the 'Second Red Scare', lasting from just after the war to the mid-1950s, gave birth to McCarthyism: the irrational fear that Soviet agents were clandestinely subverting the American government and institutions. Robert J, Goldstein, in 'Prelude to McCarthyism: The Making of a Blacklist', *Prologue* magazine (Washington DC, National Archives and Records Administration), explains:

> It originated with President Truman's Executive Order 9835 of March 21, 1947, which required that all federal civil service employees be screened for 'loyalty.' The order specified that one criterion to be used in determining that 'reasonable grounds exist for belief that the person involved is disloyal' would be a finding of 'membership in, affiliation with or sympathetic association' with any organization determined by the attorney general to be 'totalitarian, Fascist, Communist or subversive' or advocating or approving the forceful denial of constitutional rights to other persons or seeking 'to alter the form of Government of the United States by unconstitutional means.'

For McCarthy and adherents of his philosophy, Washington's apathy was an open invitation for the DPRK to invade the south. Secretary of State Dean G. Acheson, however, while focusing on Soviet activities, either direct or by proxy, in Europe, did not drop Korea from his radar. And behind the scenes, by late 1946, a CIA antecedent, the Office of Reports and Estimates (ORE), refined its operational functions by introducing the meaningful and popular *Daily Summary*, *Weekly Summary*, *Review of the World Situation* and *Intelligence Highlights*, the latter used by the DCI (Director of Central Intelligence) to disseminate both important and critical information to selected key recipients in the administration and the military.

Up until the outbreak of hostilities, there were very few CIA officers in Korea. This was further evidence that the State Department and the military were not yet convinced of the possibility of communist aggression across the 38th. The majority in Truman's administration treated Korea as an inconsequen-

AMERICANS.....
DON'T PATRONIZE REDS!!!!

——•——

YOU CAN DRIVE THE REDS OUT OF TELEVISION, RADIO AND HOLLYWOOD.....

THIS TRACT WILL TELL YOU HOW.

WHY WE MUST DRIVE THEM OUT:

1) The REDS have made our Screen, Radio and TV Moscow's most effective Fifth Column in America ... 2) The REDS of Hollywood and Broadway have always been the chief financial support of Communist propaganda in America ... 3) OUR OWN FILMS, made by RED Producers, Directors, Writers and STARS, are being used by Moscow in ASIA, Africa, the Balkans and throughout Europe to create hatred of America ... 4) RIGHT NOW films are being made to craftily glorify MARXISM, UNESCO and ONE-WORLDISM ... and via your TV Set they are being piped into your Living Room—and are poisoning the minds of your children under your very eyes ! ! !

So REMEMBER — If you patronize a Film made by RED Producers, Writers, Stars and STUDIOS you are aiding and abetting COMMUNISM .. . . every time you permit REDS to come into your Living Room VIA YOUR TV SET you are helping MOSCOW and the INTERNATIONALISTS to destroy America ! ! !

American anti-communist literature during the McCarthyism era of the 1950s.

tial backwater, to the extent that CIA reports from Korea only met the needs of 'lower-level customer demands'. Such reports were adjudged of insufficient priority to disseminate within the higher policy-making echelons. The monthly *Review* was generally not circulated outside of the NSC inner circle, so due to the fact that Truman only started to attend NSC meetings after the invasion, he was not in a position to formulate his own views about what might be happening – if anything – in Korea.

By November 1948, circulation of the *Review* had expanded to reach twenty-four government and military offices, including the White House. This development, however, did very little to impact on Far East policies. Korea was viewed as just another one of several Soviet-sponsored Cold War strategies to test the West's response, but at this time, focus was on the ideological rift in Germany that threatened to plunge Europe into the crucible of a third global conflict. From 1947 to 1950, ORE started to draw attention to a possible crisis in the Korean Peninsula's future.

33 DEAD IN KOREAN RIOTING

U.S. Forces Placed on Alert

A San Francisco message says that Ray Falk, broadcasting from Seoul, Korea, said 33 persons had been killed and 42 wounded in the past three days during rioting in South Korean provinces.

Falk said Communists had stormed police stations with the object of discrediting the United Nations. American forces stationed on the 38th parallel separating the Russian and American areas had been placed on the alert as sniping was expected, and patrols had been increased.

The broadcaster said the Americans had been ordered not to become involved in any demonstrations as trouble was anticipated during today's Korean celebrations.

Messages from Seoul, capital of Korea, report that American troops are digging in along the border dividing Korea into American and Soviet occupation zones, according to New Delhi Radio.

Nottingham Journal, Monday, 1 March 1948

The February 1948 *Review* indicated that Korean nationalists were becoming increasingly frustrated over the apathy and procrastination to facilitate the general elections that would provide the necessary legal mandate to a unified independent Korea – this had been promised.

GI waiting to board a C-47 transport for Korea. (Photo US Army)

In March, intelligence on the ground prompted the CIA to contend that evidence of increasing polarization on opposite sides of the 38th Parallel pointed toward the formation of two antagonistic regimes. In such a scenario, the south would be defeated in the event of an invasion from the communist north – with Moscow's full permission.

In the aftermath of the south-only elections, ORE reported on major political rivalry in the south with ongoing meddling by Moscow. The intelligence body believed that the US could not afford to withdraw its troops until such time that the ROKA had been equipped and trained to a level where it would be capable of severing its dependence on the Americans. The imminent victory of communist forces in China added a further worrying dimension to an already volatile situation.

In the February 1949 *Review*, the CIA was ringing the alarm bells – the peninsula would face a major hiatus should the American withdrawal happen prematurely:

> it is doubtful if the Republic could survive a withdrawal of US troops in the immediate future. [In the absence of a US military presence] it is highly probable that northern Korea alone, or northern Koreans assisted by other Communists, would invade southern Korea and subsequently call upon the USSR for assistance. Soviet control or occupation of Southern Korea would be the result.
>
> Withdrawal of US forces from Korea in the spring of 1949 would probably in time be followed by an invasion, timed to coincide with Communist-led South Korean revolts, by the North Korean People's Army possibly assisted by small battle-trained units from Communist Manchuria. Although it can be presumed that South Korean security forces will eventually develop sufficient strength to resist such an invasion, they will not have achieved that capability by the spring of 1949. It is unlikely that such strength will be achieved before January 1950. Assuming that Korean Communists would make aggressive use of the opportunity presented them, US troop withdrawal would probably result in a collapse of the US-supported Republic of Korea, an event that would seriously diminish US prestige and adversely affect US security interests in the Far East. In contrast, continued presence in Korea of a moderate US force would not only discourage the threatened invasion but would assist in sustaining the will and ability of the Koreans themselves to resist any future invasion once they had the military force to do so and, by sustaining the new Republic, maintain US prestige in the Far East.
>
> Quoted by Dr Clayton Laurie, Center for the Study of Intelligence

The departments of State, Navy, and Air Force, took full cognizance of the report, but the Intelligence Division of the army, long-time proponents of American troop withdrawal, dissented from the prevailing consensus. The army held that an invasion was only a possibility and not a certainty. A continued US military presence would constitute 'only a relatively minor psychological contribution to the stability of the Republic of Korea'. At the time of the ORE report, the US military strength in South Korea had dropped dramatically from 40,000 to a paltry 8,000, who were shipped to occupied Japan in June 1949.

Based on intelligence gathered in mid-May 1950, the 19 June ORE report – ORE 18-50 – described North Korea as a 'firmly controlled Soviet satellite that exercises no independent initiative ... its main external aim of extending control over southern Korea'. However, it still believed that war was not imminent, despite

> the present program of propaganda, infiltration, sabotage, subversion, and guerrilla operations against southern Korea. The ultimate local objective of the Soviet Union and of the northern Korean regime, is the elimination of the southern Republic of Korea and the unification of the Korean peninsula under Communist domination.

Ironically, and perhaps tragically, the report noted a build-up of DPRK troops, artillery and tanks along the 38th Parallel, together with the evacuation of the local populace along the line. Other than that, ORE stated that the situation in the whole of Korea had changed little.

At the commencement of the invasion, the comparative strengths were:

	DPRK	ROK
Infantry divisions	10 divisions (30 regiments) 5 divisions from Red China (most high-ranking officers from USSR and China)	8 divisions (22 regiments) 1 artillery battalion per division (91 pieces)
Tank units	1 tank brigade 242 T-34 tanks Self-propelled artillery Mechanized Infantry Regiment (560 sidecars)	none (27 armoured cars)
Air Force	1 air division 211 airplanes 4 AK-9 and Il-10	8 liaison planes 14 training craft
Navy	30 vessels 3 bases	28 vessels 5 bases
Total strength	ground: 182,860 naval: 13,700 air: 2,000	ground: 95,000 naval: 8,800 air: 1,800

Source: *The Korean War 1950–53*, Kim Chum-kon, (Seoul, Kwangmyong Publishing 1980)

2. SIMMERING TENSIONS

The Cheju-do Rebellion of 3 April 1948, was a seminal event in the immediate pre-invasion history of the Korean peninsula. With the departure of the Japanese in August 1945, the 50-mile-long Korean Cheju Island, 60 miles off the southerly point of the peninsula, came under the control of the People's Committees and Committees for the Preparation of Korean Independence. The anti-right organization enjoyed a close association with the poor on the island, a sector of the population that they understandably found easy to influence ideologically. Anxious to impose its authority, the US military government established the 9th Constabulary Regiment on the island in the autumn of 1946. However, this merely served to expose the 'foreign' US administration's vulnerability in a country of which they knew very little.

As the March First, or Sam-il, Movement Memorial Day – celebrated to commemorate the public dissent against Japanese rule on 1 March 1919 – on Cheju was approaching, an extra 1,700 police were deployed from the mainland. In a tense, highly volatile situation, a group of nervous policemen fired on demonstration spectators, killing six and wounding six. In a separate incident later that day, elements of the constabulary also

DISTURBANCES IN KOREA

Mob Enter the Dead Emperor's Palace
Shanghai, March 7
During the funeral ceremonies of the late Emperor [Gwangmu] of Korea, serious disturbances occurred throughout the country. They were partly occasioned by emotional feeling, and partly due to a belief that the Paris [Peace] Conference has sanctioned the independence of Korea. Thousands of Koreans paraded the streets of Seoul on March 1, and hundreds forced their way into the palace where the late Emperor was lying in state. The intruders clamoured for the independence of Korea.

An Osaka message, giving further details, says disturbances and rioting are reported from several up-country towns.

The Governor-General has issued a proclamation announcing that Japan is not abandoning her suzerainty over Korea, and urging Koreans and Japanese to unite when the nation is endeavouring, in co-operation with the other Powers, to establish a permanent peace in the world. – Reuter.

Yorkshire Evening Post, Tuesday, 18 March 1919

Juxtaposed images taken at a ceremony in Korea in September 1945 as the Japanese flag is replaced with that of the United States. (Photo US NARA)

fired on a crowd, killing two and wounding another six. The Cheju-do Committee of the South Korea's Workers' Party immediately confronted the military government by calling a general strike. Extortion and corruption by exploitative right-wing organizations on the island were added to the committee's dissatisfaction with the American government on the island.

On the day itself – 3 April – activists attacked eleven of the island's twenty-four police posts and any property whose occupants were pro-American. By the 28th, constabulary regimental commander, Lieutenant Colonel Kim Ik-yŏl, had managed to resolve the unrest by agreeing to a peaceful settlement with the rebels. The US military government, however, would have none of it; appeasement did not appear in its lexicon of ways to deal with rebels. They were adamant that the insurrection was communist-inspired, and would therefore not sit around the table with them. Seoul tightened its control of the island, bolstering security measures and shuffling constabulary leadership. In the 10 May general election, the results from the violence-torn Cheju-do were declared null and void.

Following the assassination of the 9th Regiment commander, Lieutenant Colonel Pak Chin-gyŏng, in September, the military government conducted another operation to eliminate the rebels. The administration was also transforming the constabulary regiments into military ones, and as part of the process the 14th Regiment prepared for a tour of duty to Cheju-do. In an unforeseen development, however, the regiment, based in Yŏsu and Sunch'ŏn, mutinied. For the military, absolute and forceful repression of dissent and insurgency now remained as the only workable solution, regardless of the consequences. They resorted to virtual scorched-earth methods to achieve their objectives. Fortifications went up along the coastline, and all mountains three miles from the sea were declared subverted enemy zones, and therefore subjected to 'shoot-without-question' rules. Civilians domiciled in these areas were forced to leave and their homes razed to the ground. The 9th Regiment was pulled out and the 2nd deployed from the mainland. Combined air, ground and naval operations commenced to flush out insurgents, while walls were erected around villages on the coast to deny the rebels access to the local populace. Eventually, around 50,000 civilian guards would be sent in to comb the mountains for rebel hideouts, an exercise that was very successful and resulting in the killing of rebel leader Yi-Tŏk-gu.

The Cheju-do Rebellion ended in August 1949, but the fallout would impact on the fledgling Rhee government and the US military occupation forces for a very long time. Fatalities from the purge vary considerably, from the official figure of 27,719, to the Cheju governor's estimate of 60,000. Government archival documents reveal that more than 39,000 houses were destroyed, and as many as 400 complete villages demolished. It also cost the US military and the civilian administration dearly in terms of credibility. Conversely, it added to the DPRK's justification for an invasion.

In March 1948, the UN was thrown into disarray when, upon hearing of the Soviet-influenced Korean rejection of the UN Commission for the Unification and Rehabilitation of Korea's elections proposals, Philippine delegate Arrans voiced his deep frustration and anger at Moscow, stating, 'we may possibly find it convenient to use the atom bomb to blow up the obstruction created by Russia.' The Soviets responded by declaring that the North Koreans had merely drafted a constitution out of 'popular discontent' with the constitution promulgated in South Korea the previous year. There was no agenda to install a separate government north of the 38th.

In the weeks building up to the 10 May 1948 election, Moscow was relatively tacit, commenting only that the South Koreans despised Syngman Rhee and that North Korea was progressing well. P'yŏngyang, on the other hand, called on all Koreans to destroy the UN commission and expel the Americans from the peninsula. In anti-election propaganda and rhetoric, the north described it as 'country ruining' and all part of an ongoing US programme to shore up a corrupt and weak Rhee regime. They commended Russia's vanguard in the march forward 'under the banner of peace' and against 'the militarism of the United States'. The struggle was for a 'peaceful unification of our fatherland'.

Following the elections that brought Rhee to power in South Korea, Moscow attacked the ballot for being a travesty of American-orchestrated 'falsification, bribery and police terror'. The Soviet state news agency TASS called on the south to rise up against 'American colonization', the 'puppet government' of Syngman Rhee, and the UN commission. Rhee, admitting himself that more than 100 election candidates had been arrested just prior to the voting, was labelled the 'traitor to the Korean people' and likened to Chiang Kai-shek and Tito, a collaborator with the Japanese and 'servant of the Americans'.

The Republic of Korea's first president, Syngman Rhee.

In the third week of June, the DPRK launched a second major propaganda campaign, aimed primarily at the peoples of South Korea, vilifying Rhee and calling on them to heed the call for a 'democratic front', expel the UN Commission and participate in the prosperity of the north.

On the mainland guerrilla insurgencies had been occurring since November 1948, when more than 1,000 Yŏsu rebels, in the extreme south of the peninsula, joined other insurgents in the nearby Chiri Mountains. Their presence was difficult to detect, the numbers fluctuating considerably as the cadres continually switched between their subversive activities and lives as ordinary citizens. The CIA estimated their numbers at between 3,500 and 6,000. While some carried firearms of American and Japanese origin, many were only armed with clubs and bamboo spears.

Members of the KMAG believed that the strategy of these guerrilla groups was being determined by the DPRK as part of their destabilization programme of the south. In the Chŏlla and Kyŏngsang provinces, traditionally noted for extreme leftist activities, the ground roots-based people's committees had become so powerful in these two rich, rice-producing provinces, that in South Chŏlla the government no longer controlled the countryside outside the main towns and cities. High stone or sandbagged walls protected police posts, and dusk-to-dawn curfews were imposed. In North Kyŏngsang, where relations between the police and the populace were at flashpoint, the city of Taegu was tightly protected and curfewed. The ancient Korean capital at Kwangju, according to a US vice-consul on a fact-finding mission to the southern ROK provinces, was 'a mountainous area infested by communists who hide in the hills and make frequent raids on the villages'. A similar US military survey conducted in North Kyŏngsang in July 1949, reported:

> Small attacks and ambushes punctuated by larger attacks characterized almost every locale. Police boxes were barricaded to the roof, trees everywhere were cut down within 100 meters of the roads, local officials and policemen felt compelled to move nervously from house to house at night.

Typical of guerrilla tactics, the gangs were mainly active at night, especially when away from their mountain refuges. Police posts were the prime targets, not only because of their hatred of the constabulary, but also because that is where records of leftist individuals and their families were kept.

South Korean student soldiers, P'ohang.

American intelligence could find no direct link between the guerrillas in the south and the Soviet Union or DPRK, unlike in the northern Kangwŏn Province and along the coast of North Kyŏngsang, where the North Koreans were actively supporting the guerrilla movements, supplying arms and equipment. Toward the end of September 1949, KMAG chief, Brigadier General William Roberts, stressed to Washington that the elimination of the internal guerrilla menace had become an imperative to stabilize the ROK's way forward. He requested extra infantry officers to work with the ROKA: the capabilities of the ROKA divisions along the 38th Parallel were being compromised by the need to appropriate manpower and resources from border defence to anti-insurgency operations.

In Roberts's subsequent assessment, the US-aided campaign against the guerrillas was a success, breaking the 'backbone of the guerrilla movement'. According to the brigadier general, 6,000 guerrillas had been killed from November 1949 to March 1950. By the spring of 1950, Rhee's forces also had a satisfactory measure of success against the southern anti-government guerrillas. This too, however, was only achieved by redeploying ROKA troops away from the 38th.

For Secretary of State Dean Acheson, Rhee's mettle at dealing with the internal crisis was a critical test for his new regime. In terms of body counts, Rhee had fared well, but the whole guerrilla underground network could not be totally neutralized. There was always a danger of South Korea becoming, in the eyes of the free international community, another Kuomintang or 'little China'.

BRITISH EXPERTS' BIG ATOMIC ADVANCE

The Ministry of Supply announce that for the first time Britain has produced plutonium – the fissile element which can be used for creating atomic power. This is one of the most important steps forward in the country's atomic energy programme, says the Ministry.

The plutonium was made at the Ministry of Supply atomic research establishment at Harwell. It is extracted from a uranium slug which has been irradiated for several months in gleep [graphite low energy experimental pile], the low power atomic pile.

Because of the low power at which gleep operates the amount of plutonium is small, but it is sufficient for investigating the chemical and chemical engineering problems which will be met in the large-scale handling of plutonium.

Plutonium, which can only be produced in quantity in an atomic pile, does not exist naturally on the earth. It was first produced in quantity in 1942, in America, and being fissile can be made to break up and give out great energy.

The separation of plutonium and unused uranium from the fission products is a difficult and complicated process owing to the presence of many different radioactive elements. The final product is in the form of a solution of plutonium salt.

Plutonium was the explosive that devastated Nagasaki. It can be used either as a nuclear fuel in industry or in the production of bombs.

Harwell research station is purely for experimental work and production of plutonium will be carried out in Sellafield, Cumberland.

Dundee Courier, Monday, 7 March 1949

During a visit to Moscow in March 1949, DPRK leader Kim-Il-sung concluded a ten-year 'economic and cultural' treaty with the Soviet Union, represented by Foreign Minister Andrei Vyshinsky. Whilst the treaty was ostensibly to guarantee Moscow a privileged position in the North Korean economy, during his visit, Kim met with Stalin, at which time it is believed that Kim sought the Soviet leader's endorsement for a plan to launch an attack across the 38th. Historians and political analysts contend that a subsequent Soviet–Korean defence pact was not to allay South Korea's fears of an imminent attack by the DPRK.

Instead, it provided Moscow with a mechanism to sponsor a secret, mutual-defence treaty between the communist-run People's Republic of China (PRC) and the DPRK, the latter under Soviet protection. A member of an organization within the Nationalist Chinese government revealed a key element of the pact:

Communist China would be obliged to defend North Korea from any form of aggression. An attack on either of the two parties signatory to the treaty would be repulsed by

Romanticized North Korean propaganda poster.

joint action; and Communist China would supply North Korea with weapons, material, and military personnel from Manchuria and northern China during the period from 1 July 1949 to 30 August 1950.

Stalin mistrusted Mao Zedong – in fact he did not trust anyone including, in his own words, himself. The ageing Soviet leader had no desire to see Red China usurp his sphere of influence in North Korea, and indeed, the region. By negating any possible link between the communist state and the US, Stalin was hopeful of a pro-Soviet Peking (Beijing) that, in terms of the defence pact, would make China the principal antagonist against the US in a war on the peninsula. In equal measure, a unified pro-Peking Korea would provide a useful buffer from the large American occupying force in Japan, perceived by Mao as a threat. A North Korean invasion of the south would therefore also suit China. As late as January 1950, Washington was still sending out messages that they would only fight to defend Japan, Okinawa and the Philippines. Truman made it clear that Nationalist Chiang Kai-shek should expect no military intervention from the US if the communists attacked the nationalist hold on Formosa (Taiwan). Backing up his president, Secretary of State Dean Acheson bluntly declared that the 'new nations of Asia' were on their own. He added that both the ROK and Formosa fell outside American defence zones in the region. The communists – Soviets, North Koreans and Red Chinese – were emboldened by Washington's declared foreign policy on the Far East.

A year earlier, Stalin was strengthening his relationship with – and hold over – the DPRK. He dispatched General Terentil Shtykov to P'yŏngyang, as both ambassador to North Korea and as chief of a special military mission of forty top Soviet military leaders. Included in the high-ranking party were armoured-warfare experts, generals Katukov and Kubanov, and intelligence expert, Admiral Zakharov. Having inspected Korean troops stationed in Manchuria, the delegation continued to P'yŏngyang to begin their main objective: to modernize the KPA in twelve months, so that by June 1950, and with the re-incorporation of Korean troops fighting at the time under the Red Chinese standard in Manchuria, the KPA would be adequately prepared to cross the 38th. In February 1950, Moscow and Peking entered into a thirty-year 'Friendship Alliance and Assistance Agreement'.

The summer of 1949 was also characterized by a series of engagements on the 38th with elements of the KPA, events that would be partly causal for the invasion a year later. The first such 'battle' started on 3 May when KPA forces struck across the 38th near Kaesŏng, thirty-five miles northwest of Seoul. Over the four days that it took for the ROKA to repel the invaders, the KPA lost 400 men and ROKA twenty-eight. More than a hundred civilians also perished in the fighting. Of profound concern was the defection of two ROKA companies – of the six companies and several battalions committed – to the north, where they laid down their arms. Only half of them would return.

Boeing B-29 Superfortresses on Okinawa. (Photo USAF)

On a quiet Sunday morning, 5 June 1949, a fierce exchange took place between the two sides after North Koreans crossed the 38th in the remote Ongjin Peninsula on the west coast. UN observers were dispatched, arriving in the area on an ROK naval vessel. After being guided around by ROKA troops, the UN personnel reported to Seoul that North Korea had been the aggressor.

The worst of the border engagements, which had resulted in a large amount of fighting, occurred early in August when elements of the KPA attacked ROKA units based on a small mountain north of the 38th. Disturbed by the escalation in border engagements initiated by the north, a concerned US Ambassador Muccio reported to Washington (quoted *Korea, the Unknown War* by Halliday & Cumings):

Captain Shin stated that the reports from Ongjin reaching military headquarters on the morning of August 4 were most alarming. These reports indicated that the [South] Korean forces on the [Ongjin] peninsula had been completely routed and that there was nothing there to stand against the northern onslaught. He went on that in studying the situation with the general staff ... the military were insistent that the only way to relieve pressure on Ongjin would be to drive north. The military urged mounting an immediate attack north towards Charwon [Cholwon].

In line with the advice given by General Roberts [KMAG], Captain Shin decided against attack and took immediate steps to send limited reinforcements into Ongjin.

Captain Shin went on that as soon as the Prime Minister [Yi Pŏm-sŏk] returned from the Rhee-Chiang meeting ... he called Captain Shin and remonstrated with him that he should have had more courage, should have attacked the North. That General Lee [Pŏm-sŏk] took this position does not surprise me especially. It did surprise me, however, when Captain Shin went on to say that upon his return from Chinhae the following day President Rhee also told him that he should not have decided against attacking Charwon.

In a second memorandum on 16 August, Muccio wrote of a meeting he had had over the Ongjin incident with Rhee:

[Rhee] threw out the thought that ... he might replace [Chief of Staff] Ch'ae [Pyŏng-dŏk] with General Kim Suk Wan [Kim Sŏk-wŏn] ... Kim Suk Wan has long been a favorite of President Rhee. Last fall, prior to Yŏsu, Rhee mentioned to General Coulter and myself that Kim had offered to 'take care of the North' if he could be supplied with 20,000 rifles for Korean veterans of the Japanese Army, who were burning with patriotism. The Minister of Defense, the Korean general staff and American advisers are all against General Kim. They do not consider him a good soldier but a blusterer. They have called my attention to his propensity for needling northern forces in his sector of the front, for resorting to Japanese banzai attacks and for deploying all his forces in a most hazardous manner right on the front without adequate reserves. They particularly object to his ignoring headquarters and going direct to President Rhee.

Tensions on both sides of the 38th Parallel progressively increased. Through their ambassador in Seoul, Washington was well aware that further provocation from the north might be the final catalyst to precipitate a South Korean invasion of the north. And while Kim Il-sung's plans were not totally clear, such a unilateral act by the south could become a dangerous possibility. Muccio again apprised Washington of the situation at the end of August:

There is increasing confidence in the Army. An aggressive, offensive spirit is emerging. Nerves that were frayed and jittery the past few months may now give way to this new spirit. A good portion of the Army is eager to get going. More and more people feel that the only way unification can be brought about is by moving north by force. I have it from Dick Johnston [a *New York Times* reporter] that Chiang Kai-shek told Rhee that the Nationalist air force could support a move north and that they discussed the possibility of the Nationalists starting an offensive move against Manchuria through Korea!

Marching Nationalist Chinese troops in the Jiangsu or Yunnan Province. (Photo Arthur Rothstein)

There is some feeling that now is the time to move north while the Chinese communists are preoccupied. I doubt whether Rhee would actually order a move north in his saner moments. Captain Shin, I know, is dead against it. Lee Bum Suk [Yi Pŏm-sŏk] would love it. However, should we have another Kaesong or Ongjin flare-up, a counter-attack might lead to all sorts of unpredictable developments.

Roberts had in fact ordered the ROKA commanders not to attack, warning that the US would withdraw its advisors if he was ignored. British sources at the time were quoted as saying that the ROKA commanders' 'heads were full of ideas of recovering the North by conquest'. Journalist A. T. Steele, writing on October 1949, said:

An unadmitted shooting war between the governments of the US and Russia is in effect today along the 38th Parallel. It is smoldering throughout the territory of the new Republic of Korea ... only American money, weapons, and technical assistance enable [the Republic] to exist for more than a few hours. [The ROK] was dedicated to liberty ... a tight little dictatorship run as a police state. Once the American props are withdrawn, South Korea will fall beneath the weight of communist Asia.

A final deflection away from thoughts of a North Korean invasion in 1950 came in the form of increased focus on Taiwan. British intelligence services believed that Chairman Mao's final 'battle' of the Chinese civil war against the nationalists would take place in June 1950 with the communist Chinese invasion of Taiwan. The British Foreign Office concurred, based on intelligence from two of their high-ranking members of staff, Donald Maclean and Guy Burgess. The latter had been appointed to the Far East Department in 1948. This was before it was discovered that Burgess, cryptonym Hicks, had been a member of a Soviet spy ring in the UK – the Cambridge Five – since the Second World War. Burgess informed London that Mao's invasion of Formosa would occur in either May–June or September–October. Was Burgess a player in a diversionary ploy in preparation for the DPRK's invasion of the south?

In the autumn of 1949, a group of Americans organized an unofficial military advisory group to assist the nationalists with the defence of Taiwan. Leading members of the group were William Pawley, former US ambassador and entrepreneur with nationalist Chinese business links, and Admiral Charles Cooke, staunchly anti-Chinese Communism commander of US Naval Forces in the Western Pacific.

Right up to the eve of the DPRK invasion, more and more individuals in the American diplomatic and intelligence organs were becoming convinced that Chiang Kai-shek's regime was under immediate threat from either an invasion from Mao's forces or from an internal coup by nationalists dissatisfied with Chiang. US consul in Taipei, Robert Strong, dispatched a terse cable on 17 May: 'Fate of Taiwan sealed, communist attack can occur between June 15 and end July'. The very next day, the US consulate in the Taiwanese capital informed Washington that the consensus at a meeting of 'all American representatives', Taiwan would be attacked by 15 July at the latest.

MACLEAN 'WARNED': BEAT M.I.5. BY HOURS

Atlee Ordered His Arrest 4 Years Ago

Official confirmation by the Foreign Office that Donald Maclean and Guy Burgess, the two missing diplomats, had been Soviet spies for many years when employed in high-ranking posts in the Foreign Office, did not come as a surprise to informed circles. But strict security consideration prevented the disclosures of some details which can now be told.

I can reveal that Mr. Atlee, then Prime Minister, ordered the arrest of Maclean in May, 1951, after a report from Sir Percy Sillitoe, then Director of the Military Intelligence Department (the so-called M.I. 5) was submitted to him.

For a considerable period, security officers had been watching Maclean and established that he was in regular, though indirect, contact with the first secretary of the Soviet Embassy, Mr. Feodor Kislitzin. This contact Maclean maintained with the help of go-between agents, some of whom were known to the British Secret Service.

But Maclean and his contact men worked so cleverly that M.I. 5 counter espionage agents were unable to provide sufficient evidence that any Foreign Office documents had actually been passed on by Maclean to his Soviet masters.

However, in May 1951, Commander Leonard Burt of the Special Branch and officers of M.I. 5 had finally accumulated sufficient material to warrant Maclean's arrest on the grounds that he had infringed the Official Secrets Act in his capacity as a civil servant.

It is said that high Foreign Office officials were against such a move, because it might have compromised the foreign service in the eyes of the world, and particularly in the United States. The Foreign Office was then conducting delicate negotiations with the United States Government about the sharing of atomic secrets, which America refused to impart to Britain. But Mr. Atlee decided to accept Sir Percy Sillitoe's advice and he empowered him to ask the Director of Public Prosecution to start proceedings against Maclean.

Burgess, though regarded as unreliable, was not then known as a spy, and there was no intention of arresting him. Burgess had an extensive knowledge of Russian affairs, and was often consulted on draft replies to Moscow's notes. Maclean was tipped off by some person unknown, but one who must have had access to Secret Service sources, that his arrest was imminent.

Maclean persuaded Burgess to escape too, apparently thinking he might talk.

[The two men escaped to France on 25 May 1951. Both died in Moscow, Burgess in 1963 and Maclean in 1983.]

Lancashire Evening Post, Monday, 19 September 1955

In London, Burgess was intercepting and studying every communication coming in from Taipei, and it was noted in the Soviet press that an inordinate amount of column space was being taken up by information on events in Taiwan. On 24 June, the Soviet spy, from the comfort of his office in London, concluded that the Kremlin had now accepted that US foreign policy did not support any form of US involvement in Taiwan if it was invaded by communist forces from the mainland.

In that last weekend of June 1950, Washington woke up to a languid summer's day. President Truman was enjoying a relaxing break at his home in Independence, Missouri, while Secretary of State Acheson had escaped the rigours of office to his Sandy Spring country farm.

At first light on Sunday morning, 25 June, everything in the Far East was turned on its head, but despite all the certainty from across the globe, the crisis did not erupt in Taiwan.

A refugee family in South Korea, a problem that would assume epic proportions. (Photo via defenseimagery.mil)

3. STRENGTHS AND WEAKNESSES

North Korea

In May 1950, American intelligence rated northern and southern forces 'nearly equal' in terms of training, internal leadership and combat readiness, asserting that the DPRK possessed superior armour, aircraft and artillery capabilities. Long-term operational sustainability, however, would be entirely dependent on an increase in the level of logistical support from Moscow.

It would be highly unlikely that the Soviets would commit any of its own forces, for fear of a more global conflict. Moscow's interest in a secure North Korea was largely geographic, and to a much lesser extent, economic. The close proximity – eighty miles – of the port of Vladivostok to the DPRK border gave the USSR significant added secondary air and naval base options beyond the remote fringes of the Soviet Far East. The imperative for Moscow, therefore, was a completely stable communist government in Korea, propped up by a significant infusion of war matériel, and military advice and training.

At this time, 16,000 Korean troops serving in Manchuria on secondment to the Chinese PLA, were re-absorbed into the Korean People's Army (KPA), bringing its troop strength

Soviet T-34/85 tank, mainstay of the Red Army in the Second World War. (Photo Vitaly V. Kuzmin)

according to CIA estimates, to 66,000, comprising three infantry divisions and an independent brigade. Critical power would come from a unit of sixty-five Soviet-made T-34 tanks, divisional artillery equipped with 76.2mm Model 1942, or Zis-3, field guns and 122mm M1938, or M-30, howitzers. Anti-aircraft batteries would be stationed in the border areas.

The KPA troop strength was complemented by the 20,500-strong Border Constabulary (BC), a paramilitary police force originally armed with Japanese firearms. These were now fully trained as infantrymen and equipped with Soviet weapons.

Similar intelligence suggested that the Korean People's Air Force (KPAF) comprised an air regiment of 1,500, including 150 pilots. In May 1950, Washington estimated that the KPAF was equipped with thirty-five Yakovlev Yak-9 and Ilyushin Il-10 fighter aircraft, three twin-engine bombers, two twin-engine transports, and around thirty-five Japanese and Soviet trainers.

US intelligence described the Korean People's Navy (KPN) capabilities as being of 'little consequence'. Its strength was estimated at 5,100, supplemented by a little-known marine unit comprising some 5,400 men.

The DPRK relied almost entirely on the logistical support it received from the Soviet Union. The CIA had, however, also received reports that limited quantities of small arms and munitions were being manufactured locally. The DPRK economy, though, was as yet uncommitted to supplying its armed forces, resulting in a disproportionate drain on the fiscus by the communist state's expanding military machine, particularly in the less-populated northern regions.

Three weeks into the war, on 18 July 1950, the CIA revised its estimates of the DPRK's military strengths. KPA ground forces were estimated at 74,000: seven infantry divisions

Their [Soviet air force] three best-known designers are Alexander Yakovlev, Sergei Ilyushin and Andre Toupolev. Yakovlev is the designer of the Yak fighter, a single-seat fighter with a cannon firing through the propeller hub. It is with this machine that Russian pilots carry out their propeller nibbling tactics, and the whole machine is said to be surprisingly light and fast, quite equal to the Heinkels and the Messerschmitts it had to face. Yakovlev has had a name for being able to get more speed for a given horse-power than any other designer.

Toupolev has been designing heavy bombers for the Russians since 1920. It was one of his efforts that was used for the first trans-Arctic flight to America, and it was his latest effort, the TB-7 which carried M. Molotov. This machine is the standard Soviet heavy bomber about equal in size to our [RAF] Stirling. An all-metal machine, it is said to have four engines of 1,330 h.p., and the one Molotov flew in was certainly well armed. This is probably the machine the Russians use for the occasional raids on Berlin.

The Sphere, Saturday, 27 March 1943

Soviet 76mm divisional gun, ZIS-3 M1942. (Photo Vitaly V. Kuzmin)

of approximately 10,000 men each and 4,000-strong armoured brigade. From the pre-invasion estimate of 100 Soviet-made tanks – T-34/76 and T-34/85 models – it was now believed that a further 100–200 had been had been activated from stockpiles in either the DPRK or the Soviet Union.

Each division was equipped with:

18 x 122mm M1938, or M-30, howitzers
30 x 76.2mm Model 1942, or Zis-3, field guns
54 x 45mm Model 1942, or M-42, semi-automatic anti-tank guns
18 x 120mm Model 1943 'Samovar' mortars
81 x 82mm Model 1937 battalion mortars
Engagements had discovered the use of 155mm howitzers, but not as standard divisional equipment.

Of the estimated 28,000 men of the DPRK Border Constabulary (BC), some 23,000 were organized and equipped on tactical lines in the 1st, 3rd and 7th brigades. This brought the total KPA strength to 97,000, which included 20,000 Korean-Manchurian veterans who had served and fought with the Communist Chinese. In terms of leadership, many of the KPA's senior officers had been resident in the USSR before the Second World War, where they had gone on to serve in the Red Army as commissioned officers and NCOs. The only trained reserves in the DPRK were the 3rd and 7th constabulary brigades. It was also believed that there were still 70,000 North Koreans in Manchuria, constituting a strategic reserve. Beyond this, the CIA estimated that there was a 900,000-strong reservoir of physically fit men capable of taking up arms.

Estimates of the KPAF manpower strength was marginally increased to 1,700, in a reinforced division formation. The aircraft were all propeller-driven, Second World War Soviet surplus: Yakovlev Yak 7Bs or 9s, Lavochkin La-5s and -7s, and Ilyushin Il-10s.

The KPN comprised five divisions: four at Wŏnsan on the eastern Sea of Japan coast, and one at Chinnamp'o on the western Yellow Sea coast. Of the 5,495 personnel on strength, only 700 were attached to the fifty vessels that made up the KPN's capabilities. The seagoing vessels included torpedo boats, submarine chasers and minesweepers.

Kim-Il-sung's military was the exclusive product of the Soviet Union, ranging from the staff college training of commanders, down to operational advice to the battalion echelons. Washington believed that, in this regard, the ROK armed forces were at the same level. In the air, training appeared to be in its infancy, and the air force had not attained operational status. The DPRK navy barely featured in the Soviet's military budget.

A breakdown of the Soviet advisory and training programme was a reflection of where Moscow's priorities lay: the army was allocated 2,000 advisors, the air force seventy, and the navy a paltry thirty-three. There were, however, about 2,000 Soviet troops stationed in northern DPRK ports to service Russian vessels and to maintain control of port facilities.

CIA sources discovered that morale in the services was good, with very little indication of any factional issues. Draconian discipline and incessant indoctrination and surveillance, coupled with favoured rations, pay and special privileges, ensured unreserved loyalty and a powerful psychological willingness to take on the south in battle. An added plus was the presence of the former Manchurian troops, who lacked any affinity with the south, thus providing core strength to the KPA.

South Korea

On 8 September 1945, the first of the post-war US forces – the US 7th Infantry Division – arrived at the Korean west-coast port of Inch'ŏn. The following day, the unit moved to Seoul where senior commanders of the Japanese forces signed the instruments of their unconditional surrender. North of the 38th Parallel, the Soviets would perform the same act. In the absence of any formal plans for Korea's future beyond the withdrawal of the occupying Soviet and US armies, it was left to General Douglas MacArthur to put in place a temporary military administration. He appointed Lieutenant General John R. Hodge as commander of US Army Forces in Korea (USAFIK), while designating the US CCIV Corps, comprising the 6th, 7th, and 40th infantry divisions, as the occupation force.

However, Hodge's attempt to provide continuity by retaining the incumbent Korean and Japanese personnel to administer a civilian government was wholly misguided. This included General Nobuyuki Abe of the Imperial Japanese Army as governor-general. After thirty-five years under the colonial yoke of Imperial Japan, to the Koreans this was an anger-provoking insult. Truman immediately intervened, and Hodge was obliged to discard his quick fix and replace all remaining Japanese as a matter of urgency. It would then become a military government.

In November, the military administration formed an office of the Director of National Defense to control the Bureau of Police, and a new Bureau of Armed Forces, comprising army and navy departments. Hodge recommended that a 'modest' defence force be raised to augment the 25,000-strong police force. The combined army and air force would have a corps of three infantry divisions, with the necessary support and services echelons, and one transport and two fighter squadrons, with groundcrews. It was envisaged that the total strength would be 45,000, of which the navy and coast guard would be restricted to 5,000 personnel.

In Washington, it was agreed that the Korean National Police (KNP) would be issued with American weapons and equipment, thereby relieving US military forces of civil policing responsibilities. Widespread civil unrest, however, revealed weaknesses in the ability of the KNP to deal with the situation without backing from the US army. Becoming aware of these shortcomings, in December 1945, General Hodge tasked Director of National Defense, Brigadier General Arthur S. Champeny, to formulate an interim plan to address the issue. Champeny came up with a proposal, dubbed 'BAMBOO', to ultimately infantry-train 25,000 men to form a police reserve, and thereby bolster ROK's internal strength. Initially, one company would be raised in each of the country's provinces, which, over time, would be built up to constabularies of regimental strength.

American advisors to the constabulary clandestinely purloined 60,000 Japanese rifles, which Tokyo had ordered destroyed, to equip the recruits. Training was restricted to the use of small arms only and drill on the basis that they were reserves to the police and not a combat unit. However, with the objective of creating a potential nucleus for a future ROK army, US advisors trained some of the provincial regiments in the use of machine guns and mortars.

US M24 Chaffee light tank. (Photo Armchair Aviator)

A year later, training was deemed complete, and Korean Dong yul Lyh became the first head of the Department of Internal Security. De facto, however, the US 'advisors' remained in place, denying the new indigenous leaders any form of material decision-making autonomy.

Responding to a request from the US Department of the Army in October 1947, General Hodge recommended an ROK army of six divisions, trained over twelve months by 600 US military advisors. MacArthur, on the other hand, felt that any such raising of a local army should conform with the wishes of the UN. He also believed that existing training facilities would not be able to process such numbers, adding that quality Korean officer material was extremely scarce. Instead, the veteran of the Philippines had a preference for an expansion of the constabulary to 50,000.

In February 1948, only four months before the crucial general election, the KPA was born. It would be equipped by the US with infantry weapons, field artillery and armour, including the M24 Chaffee light tank.

The retention of US troops, however, remained contentious and divisive in military corridors. In January 1948, the Joint Strategic Survey Committee told the Joint Chiefs of Staff (JCS):

> Present information indicates that the withdrawal of US forces will probably result in communist domination, and it is extremely doubtful if it would be possible to build up the Constabulary in time and with facilities available ... to prevent Soviet encroachment. The eventual domination of Korea by the USSR will have to be accepted as a probability if US troops were withdrawn. However, an augmented Constabulary might be a temporary deterrent to overt acts by North Korean forces.

In April, the NSC reported to Truman that there were three Korean options available to him: turn his back on Korea, perpetuate his military and political support, or fund, train and equip the Korean military, backed up with US economic support. Truman took the third option, setting the wheels in motion for a full withdrawal of US troops by the end of 1948. Moscow declared the same deadline for the withdrawal of its own military from North Korea.

By December, when the UN called on the US to withdraw all its forces, there were still 16,000 south of the 38th. On 15 January 1949, the US XXIV Corps left for Japan to be demobbed. All that now remained were the 5th US Infantry Regimental Combat Team (RCT) and the Provincial Military Advisory Group (PMAG). MacArthur, meanwhile, continued with his indifference toward the ROK, behaviour characterized by contradictions. He insisted that the south would inevitably fall to an invasion from North Korea, but all the while maintaining that the US did not have the means in Korea to train and equip its temporary wards. This suggested that he possessed some knowledge of the Soviet-backed North Korean capabilities, yet he appeared to lack even the slightest empathy for the country he was leaving behind.

RUSSIA MAY WITHDRAW HER TROOPS

Hint in Germany

The Soviet Army hinted in print to-day that Russian may follow the same policy in Germany as in Korea and withdraw her occupation forces earlier than the Western Allies.

A front-page editorial in 'Taegliche Rundschau,' the official Soviet military organ in Berlin, asserted: 'Korea is an example for Germany – at least in so far as the attitude of the Soviet Union is concerned.'

It said that the last Russian troops had evacuated North Korea on December 25 and 'complete Korean independence in a united state could be possible but for American forces remaining in South Korea.

'The comparison between Korean developments and those in West and East Germany goes on,' the paper added.

Derby Daily Telegraph, Thursday, 6 January 1949

Early in May, the RCT left Korea, leaving only the US advisory group. On 24 August, the latter provisional agreement ended automatically, and Syngman Rhee's freshly elected South Korean government assumed full control of all its forces. The RCT left behind $40 million worth of military hardware, including small arms, machine guns, light artillery, and jeeps and light trucks.

In June 1950, the ROKA strengths, shown here, included three divisions that were considerably below establishment:

1st Division (11th, 12th, 13th regiments)	9,715
6th Division (7th, 8th, 19th regiments)	9,112
2d Division (5th, 16th, 25th regiments)	7,910
7th Division (1st, 3rd, 9th regiments)	9,698
3d Division (22nd, 23rd regiments)	7,059
8th Division (10th, 21st regiments)	6,866
Capital Division (2nd, 12th regiments)	7,061
17th Regiment	2,500
5th Division (15th, 20th regiments and 1st Separate Battalion)	7,276

On 26 June 1950, the ROKA was reorganized as follows:

ROKA headquarters	3,000
Replacement Training Command	9,016

US divisional artillery attached to the 1st ROKA Division fire a 90mm anti-aircraft gun. (Photo US Army)

Chonju Training Command	8,699
Kwangju Training Command	6,244
Pusan Training Command	5,256
3rd Division (1st Cavalry, 22nd, 23rd regiments)	8,829
ROKA non-divisional troops	11,881
I Corps (activated 5 July 1950)	3,014
Capital Division (1st, 17th, 18th regiments)	6,644
8th Division (10th, 16th, 21st regiments)	8,864
II Corps (activated 15 July 1950)	976
1st Division (11th, 12th, 15th regiments)	7,601
6th Division (2nd, 7th, 19th regiments)	5,727
Total assigned	94,570
Wounded / non-battle casualties	8,699
Total effectives	85,871
Total in divisions	37,670

Source: Tucker, Spencer C. (ed.) *Encyclopedia of the Korean War, A Political, Social, and Military History* (Checkmark Books, New York, 2002)

During its tenure in South Korea, the US military administration also created the Korean Coast Guard. A training facility was established at the former Japanese naval base at Chinhae near Pusan, and a miscellany of small US surplus vessels allocated.

At the outbreak of hostilities, the Republic of Korea Navy (ROKN) had a strength of 7,000, and a 'fleet' of seventy former US and Japanese vessels, mainly minesweepers and small patrol boats. The US-built frigate *Paektusan* was the largest. ROKN bases were established at Mukho, P'ohang, Pusan, Yŏsu, Mokp'o, Kunsan and Inch'ŏn.

At the same time, the Republic of Korea Air Force (ROKAF) comprised a total of twenty-two trainer aircraft. Late in 1948, the Army Air Unit was formed, receiving from the US ten Piper L-4 Grasshopper unarmed trainers. A further ten Stinson L-5 Sentinel liaison unarmed aircraft arrived from the US the following month. In October 1949, the ROKAF became a separate arm of the forces.

Following civil insurrection in Yŏsu-Sunch'ŏn and repeated KPA insurgencies across the border, the Seoul government appealed to Washington for fighter-bombers to give its air force real combat capabilities. The Pentagon was not prepared to consider the request favourably, ostensibly out of concern that such aircraft might be employed by the ROK in an invasion of the north, drawing the US into a war not of its own choosing.

The ROK then undertook a nationwide fundraising campaign for the acquisition of ten North American T-6 Texan aircraft from Canada. Referred to in British Commonwealth air forces as the 'Harvard', the T-6, a single-engine trainer, was used in a combat role by

A Royal Canadian Air Force Harvard Mk4, designated in the US as the T-6 Texan. (Photo André Wadman)

the Syrian and Israeli air forces during the 1948 Arab-Israeli War. Air stations were established at Taejon, Taegu, Kwangju, Kunsan and Cheju. Two days after the invasion, the ROKAF's total ordnance of 274 33lb bombs had been used up. Hand grenades were manually dropped from the twelve serviceable L-4s and L-5s.

All the while, Rhee was incessant in his requests to Washington for essential military aid. However, the Truman administration would not deviate from its stance: America's UN obligations had been fulfilled, which included setting up the army for internal security only. There would be no tanks, no howitzers and no combat aircraft.

In the US 1950 fiscus, $10.2 million had been allocated for the ROK, but this was largely for spares and maintenance. The relatively lean budget was further eroded by a spiralling downward trend in the ROK economy. In Seoul, the KMAG and US Ambassador John J. Muccio came out in support of significant increases in the level of military aid to the vulnerable nation. Muccio pressed Washington for a doubling of the 1950 vote to $20 million, while KMAG chief, Brigadier General William L. Roberts, forwarded specific requirements. Included were North American Aviation P-51 Mustang, North American T-6 Texan and Douglas C-47 Skytrain aircraft, 3in. guns for the navy, 105mm howitzers, extra machine guns and mortars, and signalling and engineering equipment – a total of $9.8 million.

As massed KPA forces crossed the 38th in different directions and places on 25 June 1950, only $1,000 worth of US aid equipment had been received by Seoul. A further shipment of spares worth $350,000 was still on the high seas.

U.S. air power would do little to delay the North Korean juggernaut. Here USAF bombers destroy rail bridges across the Han River, southwest of Seoul. (Photo via defenseimagery.nil)

4. NORTH KOREAN BLITZKRIEG

'They struck like a cobra.'

General MacArthur on the North Korean surprise attack across the 38th Parallel

At 4 a.m. on 25 June 1950, North Korean armed forces launched attacks across the 38th Parallel, in what was immediately seen as an all-out offensive against the Republic of Korea (ROK). The massed attack was initiated in the far west when KPA artillery bombarded the Ongjin Peninsula as a prelude to the advance southward four hours later of the 3rd Brigade, Border Constabulary, and the 14th Battalion, 6th Regiment.

After more than a week of only minor border incidents, the ROKA 17th Regiment, on watch on the isolated Ongjin Peninsula, with 'devastating suddenness' found themselves at the receiving end of artillery and mortar fire. P'yŏngyang, however, would maintain that the KPA position at Unpa-san had come under heavy ROKA artillery bombardment at 10 p.m. on 23 June, lasting for six hours. This was allegedly followed by an attack on the KPA by elements of the 'Fierce Tiger' unit of the 17th Regiment, led by the ruthless Kim 'Tiger Kim' Chong-won. The KPA then destroyed the South Korean assailants.

It was also a quiet morning in the Meiji building in Tokyo, headquarters of the young but hugely combat-experienced US Far East Air Force (FEAF). FEAF commander, Lieutenant General George E. Stratemeyer, had been in the States, and was, at the time, in transit on his way back, between San Francisco and Hawaii. Acting commander and commanding general of the US Fifth Air Force in Japan, General Earle E. Partridge, was also absent from Tokyo, spending the weekend with his family in Nagoya.

Back in Korea, US field advisors of the KMAG, accustomed to North Korean armed forays, were hesitant to sound the alarm that this was in fact the 'real thing'. However, when

Kaesŏng fell at 9 a.m. and amphibious landings were made on the east coast south of Kangnŭng, it became totally clear that an invasion to subjugate the ROK by force was in progress. At 9.45 a.m., Chief Warrant Officer Donald Nichols, commander of District 8, US Office of Special Investigation (OSI) in Seoul, telephoned the FEAF duty officer in Tokyo.

The news from Korea was rapidly disseminated to all FEAF units, but General Partridge was away from his home in Nagoya at the time, and only received

The innocuous 38th Parallel crossing, showing a UN convoy later in the war. (Photo US Army)

the message at 11.30 a.m. – the invasion was now almost eight hours old.

Partridge immediately grasped the gravity of what was happening across the Sea of Japan, but he was fully aware that the only responsibility for FEAF in such an eventuality was the safe evacuation of American citizens in South Korea, and then only at the behest of the ambassador in Seoul. For MacArthur, a 'safe evacuation' plan would include attacking ground, sea and air targets in support of the evacuation operation.

North Korean army 122 mm M1931 (A-19) Soviet-made field gun. (Photo US NARA)

The US air base at Itazuke (Fukuoka) on Kyūshū Island was closest to Korea. Partridge designated the commander of the 8th Fighter-Bomber Wing to head the air task force to rescue Americans from Korea. The 8th would provide fighter cover for air and

U.S. FORMING A JAP ARMY SAYS SOVIET

At a meeting of the Allied Council for Japan in Tokio to-day, the Soviet accused the U.S. of using the Japanese police force to provide the nucleus of a new Japanese Army.

Mr William Sebald (U.S. chairman), replying to this allegation, made by the Soviet member (Lieut.-Gen. Derevyanko), said the Russian statement was part of a campaign to create 'mendacious rumours and propaganda.'

Gen. Derevyanko said the Japanese police forces had been increased two and a half times since the surrender and that, according to the Japanese Finance Ministry, they now numbered 141,206 men.

It should be remembered that Japan with 17 infantry divisions totalling 200,000 men in 1925, could begin the occupation of Manchuria five years later.

'It becomes quite clear, in the light of this precedent, that the increase of the Japanese police forces, which are already very numerous, constitutes a real menace of re-establishment of the Japanese forces.'

General Derevyanko recommended that Japanese police forces should be limited to 125,000 and asked that Japanese secret police organisations should be dissolved.

The British and Chinese members on the council saw no danger of Japanese rearmament at the moment, but warned that caution should be continued to prevent Japan's re-emergence as a military Power.

Torbay Express and South Devon Echo, Wednesday, 5 January 1949

USAF Douglas
B-26 Invaders over
US-occupied Japan,
July 1950. (Photo
USAF)

water evacuation, while other wings would be called on for added air support. Transport fell under 8th Wing command, drawing from the 374th Troop Carrier Wing at Tachikawa. In addition, the 3rd Bombardment Wing staged six Douglas B-26 Invader light bombers to Ashiya Air Base near Itazuke, from where they would conduct reconnaissance and cover sorties over the seas off Korea.

At 11.30 a.m., Partridge ordered all Fifth Air Force wing commanders to complete all the deployments for the implementation of the evacuation plan, but all flights to Korea could only commence when ordered by him to do so. That afternoon, Colonel John M. Jack Price, commander of the 8th Wing, readied his own Lockheed F-80 Shooting Star and North American F-82 Twin Mustang fighters, Douglas B-26 Invaders, and twelve Douglas C-54 Skymaster and three Douglas C-47 Skytrain (RAF designated 'Dakota') transports. At 9 p.m., Price informed Fifth Air Force operations that he was ready to start the evacuation at 3.30 a.m. the following morning, the 26th.

The time difference between Seoul and Washington must be borne in mind. When the invasion commenced at 4 a.m. on Sunday 25th, it was still 2 p.m. in Washington, Saturday 24th. It was therefore 9.26 p.m. that Seoul Ambassador Muccio's news about the invasion reached the State Department. They in turn informed Truman, the Defense Department and UN Secretary-General Trygve Lie, the latter at his residence on Long Island.

Left in no doubt that this was a serious violation of the UN charter's prohibition of aggression by one state against another, Lie assured the State Department that he would call an emergency meeting of the Security Council, but first he needed to receive confirmation from the United Nations Commission on Korea (UNCOK) in Seoul. The following morning, the 25th in the US, UNCOK chief, Dr Liu Yu-won, gave Lie the confirmation

The Korean Peninsula

Siping
Huadian
Tumen
Vladivostok
USSR
Shenyang
China
Manchuria
Tonghua
Ji'an
Manp'o
Kanggye
Najin
Ch'ongjin
Anshan
Yalu River
Tunien River
Kimch'aek
Dandong
Kusong
Yŏngbyon
Hamhung
North Korea
Korea Bay
P'yŏngyang
Wŏnsan
Sea of Japan
Namp'ŏ
Taijing River
P'yŏnggyang
Haeju
38°
Ongjin
Inchon
Seoul
Kangnŭng
Wŏnju
Samch'ŏk
Yellow Sea
Ch'ŏnan
Ham River
Chŏnju
Taejŏn
Andong
Naktong River
Kunsan
South Korea
P'ohang
Taegu
Korea Strait
Mokp'o
Masan
Uisan
Pusan
Yŏsu
Kŏje-do
Tsushima
Hiroshima
Chin-do
Ashiya air base
Fukuoka
Kitakyushu
Cheju
Itazuke air base
Japan
Cheju-do
Sasebo

© DUDLEY WALL - 2017

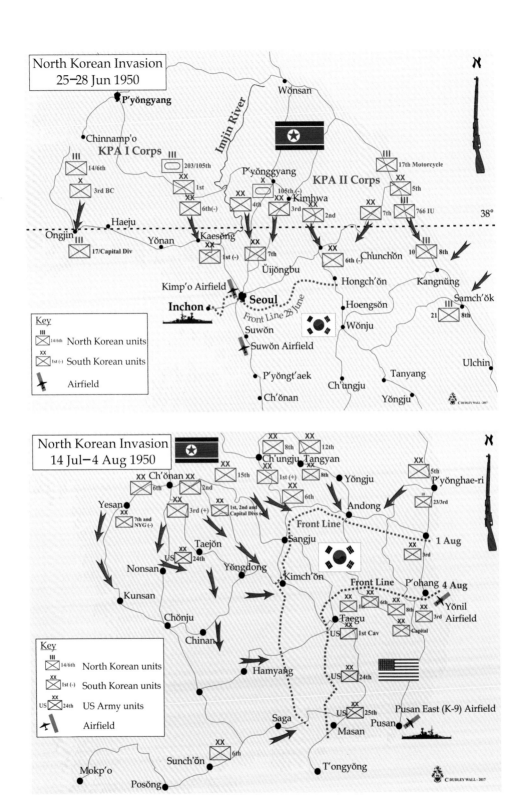

North Korean Invasion 25–28 Jun 1950

Key

North Korean units

South Korean units

Airfield

North Korean Invasion 14 Jul–4 Aug 1950

Key

North Korean units

South Korean units

US Army units

Airfield

US Air Force initial involvement in Korea

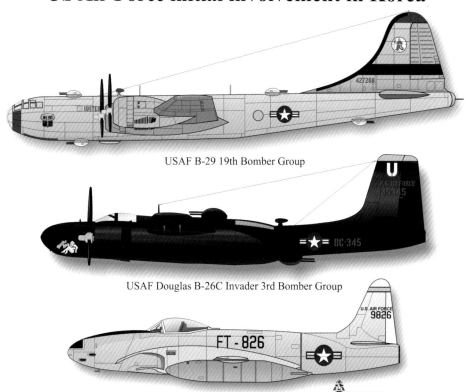

USAF B-29 19th Bomber Group

USAF Douglas B-26C Invader 3rd Bomber Group

USAF Lockheed F-80C Shooting Star 8th Fighter-Bomber Squadron

Command Pilot brevet

Far East Air Force patch

Senior Navigator brevet

5th US Air Force patch

13th US Air Force patch

20th US Air Force patch

ROK Air Force

North American F-51D of 1st Fighter Squadron

North American T-6G Mosquito

DPRK Air Force

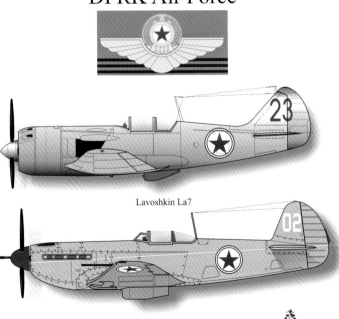

Lavoshkin La7

Yakovlev Yak-9

C DUDLEY WALL - 2017

Infantry Weapons of the Korean War

303 No 4 (Commonwealth)

Garand (USA/ROKA)

Mosin Nagant (KPA)

SKS (KPA)

M1 Carbine (USA/ROKA)

PPSh (KPA)

Thompson 45 (USA/ROKA)

Browning Automatic Rifle (USA/ROKA)

Browning 303 Machine Gun (USA/ROKA)

303 Bren Gun (Commonwealth)

C DUDLEY WALL - 2017

USAF B-26Bs of 8th Bomber Squadron, 3rd Bomber Wing. (Photo Hernandez, via Friddell)

USAF F-80Cs over Korea, 1950. (Photo USAF)

USS *Wisconsin* off the Korean peninsula. (Photo US Navy)

M24 Chaffee light tank. (Photo Balcer)

Korean War monument, Seoul. (Photo Pulgasari)

Lockheed P-80C Shooting Stars of the US 8th Fighter-Bomber Wing. (Photo USAF)

he had sought. That afternoon Lie convened a meeting of the Security Council at Lake Success, Long Island, temporary headquarters of the UN from 1946 to 1951. The council voted in favour of UN Resolution 83/1950, calling for an immediate end of hostilities, and for the DPRK to 'withdraw forthwith their armed forces to the 38th parallel'. All members of the UN were called on to 'render every assistance to the United Nations in the execution of this resolution and to refrain from giving assistance to the North Korean authorities'. The Soviet Union was absent from the meeting and Yugoslavia abstained.

Having earlier informed the president not to hurry back to Washington, Acheson again contacted Truman telling him executive decisions were now required, and requested that he return to Washington. At 7.15 p.m., Truman met with his Joint Chiefs of Staff at his temporary residence at Blair House. Present were the JCS chairman, General Omar Bradley, General J. Lawton Collins (army), Admiral Forrest P. Sherman (navy), and General Hoyt S. Vandenburg (air force). Discussions centred on the hope that the war matériel that MacArthur was sending the ROKA would stall the KPA's southward thrust.

After several exhausting hours of deliberations, Truman indicated to Acheson and his military chiefs that he would not make any quick decisions, and that he needed time to consider all options. No stranger to international conflict, and as the first person to use the atom bomb offensively, Truman's greatest concern was that the scenario had ominous undertones to the outbreak of the Second World War.

They would, however, agree on three recommendations prepared by the State and Defense departments and tabled by Acheson:

i. MacArthur to send arms and ammunition to South Korea,
ii. MacArthur would provide aircraft and ships to both protect and assist with the evacuation of American citizens from Korea,
iii. The US Seventh Fleet would be ordered to sail north from the Philippines and report to MacArthur.

At a second Blair House meeting, the JCS lifted all restrictions that would prevent FEAF from participating in full operations in the defence of the ROK south of the 38th. The Seventh Fleet would take up station to protect Taiwan from PRC invasion. In the evening of the 27th, UN Secretary-General Lie endorsed the US armed initiative, on the basis that it was 'fully within the spirit of the Council's resolution of June 25'. At Lake Success, the Security Council approved by seven votes to one (Yugoslavia opposed) a recommendation that 'Members of the United Nations furnish such assistance to the Republic of Korea as may be necessary to repel armed attack and restore international peace and security in the area'. Again, the Soviet Union's delegate, Yakov Malik, who had power of veto, chose not to attend the meeting. Was this a deliberate tactic by Stalin in an attempt to ignite an armed clash between the US and Communist China?

The USS *Missouri* anchored off the Korean coast, 1950. (Photo US Navy)

On 26 June, DPRK leader Kim made his first public comment, accusing the south of a 'general attack' north across the 38th. He claimed that Syngman Rhee had for a long time been scheming about provoking a 'fratricidal civil war'. He added that the south had conducted repeated clashes against his forces on the 38th, while colluding with Kim's sworn enemy, Japanese imperialism.

That same day, under instruction from Lie, UNCOK submitted a report on their assessment of the situation:

US sailors unload powder cans and 20.3cm shells from the cruiser USS *Toledo*, US naval base at Sasebo, Japan, 1950. (Photo US Navy)

> Commission's present view on basis is, first, that judging from actual progress of operations northern regime is carrying out well-planned, concerted and full-scale invasion of South Korea, second, that South Korean forces were deployed on wholly defensive basis in all sectors of the parallel, and third, that they were taken completely by surprise as they had no reason to believe from intelligence sources that invasion was imminent.

At the time of the commencement of the invasion, the US Eighth Army comprised four below-strength divisions: the 1st Cavalry, and the 7th, 24th and 25th infantry divisions, plus the 40th Anti-aircraft Artillery Brigade, comprising seven battalions, and a miscellany of logistic and support units. Early in 1946, the Eighth Army assumed full responsibility for the post-war occupation of the whole of Japan. Lieutenant General Walton H. Walker took over as commander in September 1948. On Okinawa, largest of the Japanese Ryukyu-Nansei Islands and 500 miles south of Korea, the US had two battalions of the 29th Infantry Regiment and two anti-aircraft brigade battalions. There were no other US units in this theatre. The 5th Regimental Combat Team (RCT) – the 'Bobcats' – had left Korea in June 1949, and were now garrisoned at Schofield Barracks in Hawaii, 4,800 miles away. Beyond that, the 'nearest' were at Camp Pendleton, California – 1st Marine Division and 1st Marine Air Wing – and at Fort Lewis, Washington – the 2nd Infantry Division. The only US military in Korea was the 492-strong KMAG.

As the morning of 25 June progressed, to the left of the KPA forces on Ongjin, the 1st and 6th divisions and the 203rd Battalion, 105th Regiment, fell on Kaesŏng. South of Pyŏnggang, in the centre of the front, the 3rd and 4th divisions and the 105th Brigade thrust across the 38th toward Ŭijŏngbu. To their left, the 2nd and 7th divisions advanced on Ch'unch'ŏn. On the eastern coastal zone, the 17th Motorcycle Regiment, the 5th Division and the 766th Independent Infantry Regiment straddled the 38th toward Kangnŭng.

Soviet-made North Korean SU-76 self-propelled artillery piece is examined by US troops, 1950. (Photo US Army)

Exploiting the element of surprise, KPA forces, led by tanks, quickly overran Ongjin and took Kaesŏng, effectively isolating the region to the west of the Imjin River and protecting the left flank of the drive on the South Korean capital, Seoul. More than fifty tanks spearheaded a column of 8–10,000 troops racing down the historical Poch'ŏn– Ŭijŏngbu corridor to the Seoul objective. On the right flank, a further column had passed through Kaesŏng and, with forty tanks, was also striking toward the capital.

Within the first few hours of the invasion, MacArthur informed State Department special representative John F. Dulles, who was working on the Japanese peace treaty in Tokyo, that the incursion by KPA forces into South Korea was not an 'all-out effort', and that the ROK military 'would gain victory'. In pursuance of the first set of instructions

The US aircraft carrier USS *Valley Forge*, seen here in Sydney Harbour, 1948. (Photo NSW archives)

A-BOMB IN KOREA: M.P.S' MOTION

The possible use of the atom bomb in Korea to which reference was made in the [British] Commons on Monday by Maj. Peter Roberts (NLU, Heeley), is the subject of a motion tabled by Mr Emrys Hughes (Lab., South Ayrshire and Mr J. Carmichael (Lab., Glasgow Bridgeton).

The motion reads, 'That this house deplore the suggestion of the member for Heeley that the Prime Minister should advise his representatives in the United Nations to ask for the use of the atomic bomb upon the capital of North Korea and welcome the statement issued by the leaders of the Opposition that this suggestion 'did not in any way represent the views of the Opposition.'

In view of this declaration, and realising that the use of the atom bomb, not only on the capital of North Korea but on all capitals and populous areas, cannot be justified either on grounds of humanity or for reasons of expediency, urges the Government to instruct their representatives at the United Nations to make new proposals for banning the atom bomb.'

Hull Daily Mail, Wednesday, 28 June 1950

---

from Washington, MacArthur had ordered the immediate dispatch of ammunition to South Korea, had placed air and naval resources on standby for the evacuation, and was waiting to give fresh orders to the Seventh Fleet that was already under sail in his direction.

While the Fifth Air Force was mobilizing an evacuation task force in Japan, by 9.30 a.m. on the 25th, it appeared to Ambassador Muccio that ROK forces were managing to prevent the KPA from entering Seoul. The main North Korean advances were tanks spearheading the 3rd and 4th KPA divisions and elements of the 105th Brigade toward Ŭijŏngbu, a town five miles north of Seoul on the main road. Further sea landings took place on the east coast between Kangnŭng and Samch'ŏk.

Around noon, the low cloud over Seoul started to lift, bringing with it the first air strikes by the Korean People's Air Force (KPAF). At 1.15 p.m., two silver Yaks buzzed the Kimp'o and Seoul airfields, obviously on a quick reconnaissance as they did not strafe the facility. However, the KPAF returned at 5 p.m. when two fighters attacked Kimp'o, scoring hits on the control tower, a fuel dump and a grounded four-engine Douglas C-54 Skymaster transport of the US Military Air Transport Service (MATS). Four other Yaks strafed Seoul Airfield, damaging seven of the ten ROKAF trainer aircraft based there, before heading north across the 38th again. At 7 p.m., six Yaks were back over Kimp'o, where they continued to pummel the C-54.

Throughout that afternoon, Muccio was incessantly badgered with calls from a desperate Syngman Rhee, begging for immediate US military hardware to withstand the

A Douglas four-engine C-54 Skymaster transport destroyed by North Korean fighters at Kimp'o Airfield, June 1950. (Photos US NARA)

North Korean onslaught: ten North American Aviation P-51 Mustangs, with bombs and rockets. ROKAF pilots were on standby at Taegu, some 150 miles southeast of Seoul – still a safe area. Unless they were received overnight for early deployment on the 26th, came the warning from Rhee, then defeat was a foregone conclusion. Rhee's other major concern was his total lack of anything to neutralize the KPA's Soviet-made T-34 tanks. He pleaded for 105mm and 155mm howitzers, and 57mm M18 recoilless rifles. With a first-hand grasp of the gravity of the situation, Muccio forwarded the requests to Tokyo and Washington, but to no avail.

As the situation threatened to worsen for Seoul that first night of the war, and the KPA tanks from Ŭijŏngbu were punching toward the capital, Muccio let MacArthur know that he was implementing the evacuation of dependent women and children from Seoul and the west-coast port of Inch'ŏn. At that time, there were a few merchant freighters docked in the harbour, which Muccio intended to use to ship the refugees around the peninsula to the Japanese port of Fukuoka.

The 8th Fighter-Bomber Wing was tasked to provide the freighters with air cover, but such a mission immediately presented the problem of distance. Long-range aircraft were needed, not the thirsty jet fighters. At Itazuke Air Base, twelve North American F-82G Twin Mustangs of the 68th Fighter All-Weather 'Lightning Lancers' Squadron were committed by unit commander Colonel Price. Numbers were augmented with the arrival at Itazuke of combat-ready F-82s from the 339th Fighter All-Weather Squadron at Yokota. However, it was still felt that the numbers of long-range fighters were still inadequate to provide strong and efficient cover. Consequently, Okinawa dispatched eight F-82Gs of 4th Fighter Squadron to Itazuke. To make room, Price was compelled to move the contingent of C-54 transports to nearby Ashiya.

By mid-afternoon on the 26th, the news from Korea reaching Tokyo was promising: Ch'unch'ŏn to the east of Seoul had been retaken and ROKA troops were standing their ground on the Ŭijŏngbu road. With no reason to question the veracity of the incoming reports, FEAF stood down the C-54s at Ayisha, releasing them to normal duties.

US 68th FAWS (Fighter All-Weather Squadron) 'Lightning Lancers' North American F-82G Twin Mustang from Itazuke Air Base, Japan. (Photo USAF)

At a meeting that afternoon between MacArthur's staff and the JCS, full approval was given to MacArthur's recommendations: the shipment of war matériel to Korea in which all ships would be protected by FEAF, and the use of force to safeguard the lives of Americans being evacuated. The meeting communicated to MacArthur the fact that the US Seventh Fleet, which included the large aircraft carrier USS *Valley Forge*, was underway to the US naval base at Sasebo, Japan.

MacArthur also needed, with some urgency, to fully understand the exact situation on the ground in South Korea. Accordingly, MacArthur tasked Brigadier General John H. Church, staff chief in MacArthur's Far East Command headquarters, to head a 'survey party' to Korea to assess the situation at the rock face, and to assess ROKA needs. Leading a party of twelve officers and two enlisted men, early in the evening of 27 June, the frail, arthritic 57-year-old Church landed at Suwŏn Airfield, twenty miles south of Seoul. The pilot had been disinclined to use Seoul's Kimp'o Airfield, for fear that the KPA had already taken the facility. By this time, the JCS had appointed MacArthur commander of all US forces in Korea, while Church's survey party was given the officious title GHQ Advance Command (ADCOM).

Upon his arrival, Church encountered a state of near chaos. Syngman Rhee's government had abandoned Seoul, and the president himself was at Suwŏn, en route to Taejŏn. The KMAG was in total disarray and had ceased to be a cohesive unit. Some had joined refugees streaming southward, while others had scattered in all directions. ROKA soldiers were adding to the congestion on the roads as they joined the refugee exodus. The bridge over the Han River at Seoul had been demolished, leaving thousands of ROKA troops and tons of military equipment stranded on the north bank.

What came as the greatest shock to Church and his fellow officers was the magnitude of the shambolic retreat of the South Korean soldiers. Contrary to popular belief in their propensity to stand and fight, the complete opposite was true: resistance was wholly absent in the area. Church attributed the calamity to the absence of leadership, the inexperienced officers having miraculously disappeared into thin air.

Koreans flee south in June 1950 after the North Korean army's invasion across the 38th Parallel. (Photo US Defense Department)

Unable to fulfil his mission by going north on any form of reconnaissance, Church effectively assumed command of the ragtag rabble that was the ROKA, and, by definition therefore, the defence of South Korea. Hours later, however, Church messaged MacArthur to inform him that the ROKA was incapable of pushing the North Koreans back, let alone stall its rapid advance. If there was any serious plan to retake Seoul, then this could only be achieved by American forces on the ground. Church returned to Japan on 14 July, before being given the command of the 24th Division on 23 July.

The first attempts at an evacuation started early on 26 June, but to the frustration of the F-82 pilots who flew non-stop relays of four at a time, it would be late afternoon before the first shipload of evacuees left Inch'ŏn. The monotony of a long, exhausting day was only broken when, at 1.33 p.m., a radial-engine North Korean fighter took on two of the F-82s. Not certain if they should retaliate, the Americans took evasive action until the enemy fighter left.

Finally, the Norwegian freighter *Reinholt*, having unloaded its cargo of fertilizer, embarked with 682 persons on board. As night set in, two F-82s continued to escort the *Reinholt* on its lumbering voyage to Japan. Eventually, US destroyers assumed the role of protector while B-26s from Japan provided air cover as the *Reinholt* headed for the harbour at Fukuoka.

The night of the 26th was, for the American expatriates in Seoul, long and stressful. At 10 p.m. President Rhee informed Ambassador Muccio that the North Korean tanks were unstoppable, and he would therefore be translocating his government to the safety of Taejon. He would do so either that very night, or at first light the following morning – the 27th. At midnight, KMAG chief, Colonel W. H. Sterling Wright, voiced his opinion to Muccio that the North Koreans would arrive in Seoul within the next forty-eight hours, galvanizing the ambassador to demand emergency evacuation measures from Tokyo. FEAF immediately commenced preparations to start the uplift at dawn on the 27th. The US Fifth Air Force would undertake escort duties, but this time

A tight formation of B-26 Invader light bombers of the US Fifth Air Force's 452nd Bomb Wing. The multiple .50in. M2 Browning machine guns can be seen in the 'all-purpose' noses of the aircraft. (Photo USAF)

KOREA SHOWS THERE IS NOT A MOMENT TO LOSE

F. M. Inwood

If the peoples of Western Europe view the civil war in Korea as a minor matter not to be compared with any of the potential sources of international trouble in this part of the world it is once again because the Allied post-war policy in the Far East has been almost exclusively American, conceived in the United States and carried out by Americans.

There was a too-ready acceptance of South Korean claims to independence and a too-willing compliance with the Korean and Russian demand for the withdrawal of occupation troops. Those who advocate the withdrawal of occupation forces from Germany have an example of the subsequent course of events when that happens.

The immediate consequences of inaction on the future course of events in Asia are incalculable. The situation is theoretically different from what has been happening in China, though in practice it is precisely the same. Since there were no recognised regions in China, the Communist attack upon Chiang Kai-shek was a revolution rather than a civil war. What has happened in Korea is a breach of the Southern boundary by Northern forces.

This Korean incident should satisfy Washington of the necessity to determine as speedily as possible to increase the size of the force it will maintain in Europe and the exact strength of the reinforcements that will be provided immediately trouble starts.

Obviously American, British and French forces will form the backbone of Western resistance either to Russian aggression or Soviet-inspired revolt in Western Europe. What those who stand in the front line of any possible trouble want to know is whether the line will hold or whether they must again be 'liberated.' We hear much of international meetings of Defence Ministers and Service chiefs but no reassuring answer to that question has yet been provided. There is no time to be lost.

In timing this Korean development for the week-end Moscow is displaying yet another feature of the Nazi technique. We must not again get into such a state of confusion that it is never safe to take a week-end off.

Nottingham Journal, Tuesday, 27 June 1950

with specific orders: 'No interference with your mission will be tolerated.' Retaliation against enemy threats had become legitimate.

On the ground at Itazuke, the orders proved problematic. Colonel Price's F-82 pilots were at their limits: one pilot had flown fifteen hours out of thirty-four. Added to this, having been stood down, the C-54s had bombshelled in different directions to resume standard duties. However, the resourceful Price wangled thirteen transports: two C-54s from the 374th Wing and eleven C-47s from the FEAF base flight and from FEAF Command. Lockheed P-80 Shooting Star jets, economical at high altitude, would provide top cover over Seoul, leaving the F-82s to orbit lower down. To strengthen his fighter capabilities, on the morning of the 27th extra aircraft from the 9th Fighter-Bomber Squadron (49th Wing) arrived at Itazuke from the home base at Komaki (Nagoya).

At dawn on the 27th, F-82s escorted the first flight of transports out of Itazuke, followed by F-80s tasked to orbit over the Han River to the south of the capital.

A USAF F-80 Shooting Star dropping what appears to be a napalm bomb over a North Korean target. (Photo US NARA)

The situation in Korea was changing by the minute. From a first estimate of 375 evacuees to be airlifted out, mainly from the Kimp'o Airfield, both KMAG and the embassy now deemed it a necessity to evacuate all non-essential staff. To achieve this, Suwŏn Airfield, twenty miles south of Seoul, would be activated as a second emergency uplift stage. UNCOK staff then swelled the number by deciding to also escape the impending danger. Despite unreliable communications hampering the accurate logistics of the airlift, by midnight of the 27th, 748 persons had been flown out of Korea to American-controlled Japan.

During the mission, that afternoon the North Koreans made it abundantly clear that they were out to destroy the American transports. Shortly after noon, five KPAF fighters arrived at 10,000 feet over Seoul. Within minutes, F-82s from the 68th and 339th Squadrons took on the Yaks, bringing down three and sending the remainder back home at full throttle. It would only be in 1953, after extensive investigations, that Lieutenant William Hudson from the 68th Fighter All-Weather Squadron was credited with the first communist kill in the air.

The second – and last – KPAF presence came later that afternoon, when eight Soviet-made Ilyushin Il-10 'Beast' ground-attack aircraft appeared over Kimp'o to attack US transports on the ground. It was, however, a mismatch, as four F-80C jet fighters of the 35th Fighter-Bomber Squadron descended on the hapless North Koreans, immediately shooting down four of their aircraft – the first USAF victories by jet fighters. The Fifth Air Force had stamped its authority over Seoul and no further KPAF aircraft returned for the rest of the evacuation mission that day.

A North Korean Ilyushin Il-10 in a damaged hangar at the Kimp'o Airfield, Seoul, Korea, 1950. (Photo US Navy)

On 27 June 1950, a concerned US President Truman made a public statement:

In Korea, the Government forces, which were armed to prevent border raids and to preserve internal security, were attacked by invading forces from North Korea. The Security Council of the United Nations called upon the invading troops to cease hostilities and to withdraw to the 38th parallel. This they have not done, but on the contrary, have pressed the attack. The Security Council called upon all members of the United Nations to render every assistance to the United Nations in the execution of this resolution. In these circumstances, I have ordered United States air and sea forces to give the Korean Government troops cover and support.

The attack upon Korea makes it plain beyond all doubt that communism has passed beyond the use of subversion to conquer independent nations and will now use armed invasion and war. It has defied the orders of the Security Council of the United Nations issued to preserve international peace and security. In these circumstances, the occupation of Formosa by Communist forces would be a direct threat to the security of the Pacific area and to United States forces performing their lawful and necessary functions in that area.

Accordingly, I have ordered the 7th Fleet to prevent any attack on Formosa. As a corollary of this action I am calling upon the Chinese Government on Formosa to cease all air and sea operations against the mainland. The 7th Fleet will see that this is done. The determination of the future status of Formosa must await the restoration of security in the Pacific, a peace settlement with Japan, or consideration by the United Nations.

I have also directed that United States Forces in the Philippines be strengthened and that military assistance to the Philippine Government be accelerated.

I have similarly directed acceleration in the furnishing of military assistance to the forces of France and the Associated States in Indochina and the dispatch of a military mission to provide close working relations with those forces.

I know that all members of the United Nations will consider carefully the consequences of this latest aggression in Korea in defiance of the Charter of the United Nations. A return to the rule of force in international affairs would have far-reaching effects. The United States will continue to uphold the rule of law.

I have instructed Ambassador Austin, as the representative of the United States to the Security Council, to report these steps to the Council.

Mid-afternoon on the 27th, MacArthur received his landmark instructions to deploy air and naval forces in support of the ROK. At 11.20 a.m., General George Stratemeyer arrived at the US Haneda Army Air Base (today Tokyo International) to resume control

A USAF B-26 Invader firing rockets at Korean rail marshalling yards, 1950. (Photo USAF)

of FEAF from Partridge. MacArthur's experiences in combat made him fully aware that immediate action was a necessity, and that, over the next thirty-six hours, FEAF had to throw everything they had at the invading North Koreans. He was convinced that rapid and robust air strikes would send the KPA scurrying back across the 38th.

Anxious not to compromise the defensive integrity of Japan, MacArthur gave Partridge the requested permission to move the 19th Bombardment Group from Guam to Kadena Air Base on Okinawa.

In Japan, the Far East Command, in the absence of a contingency to systematically deal with such a crisis in Korea, was frantically busy preparing and disseminating orders to facilitate optimum deployment. In the interim, FEAF operations officers were acting on direct verbal orders from MacArthur. One such order was for the Fifth Air Force to conduct reconnaissance sorties – photographic and visual – over Korea. Another instructed the Fifth Air Force to perform combat missions with B-26s through the night of 27/28 June. A schedule of aerial missions for the 28th ensued: the Twentieth Air Force was to move all equipped and armed B-29s from Guam to Kadena Air Base on Okinawa, from where they would conduct sorties against targets of opportunity, such as groups of tanks, artillery batteries and troop convoys; the Fifth Air Force was to deploy two squadrons of B-26s, four squadrons of F-80s and two squadrons of F-82s on aggressive strike missions against the enemy, including bridges and military traffic found between the 38th and the front line.

Late on the 27th, MacArthur gave FEAF an additional operational task. While transport by sea of ammunition from Japan to Korea would be far more efficient, an urgent bridging measure had to put in place until the beginning of July when such naval journeys would become routine. On 28 June, FEAF airlifted 150 tons of ammunition into Suwŏn from Tachikawa, western Tokyo. Thereafter, the 374th Troop Carrier Wing flew out 200 tons a day until 1 July, with escort cover provided by the 8th Fighter-Bomber Wing.

At dusk on 27 June, four RF-80s, the photo-reconnaissance version of the Lockheed F-80 Shooting Star, of the 8th Tactical Reconnaissance Squadron moved south from Yokota to Itazuke in readiness for missions over Korea the next day. Simultaneously, the 3rd Bombardment Group and the 13th Bomb Squadron transferred from Johnson Air Base (today called Iruma) northwest of Tokyo, to join 8th Squadron at Ayisha Air Base on Kyūshū.

Unfortunately, the night mission of the B-26 Invaders on 27/28 June had very limited success, due entirely to circumstances beyond their control. Of the ten 8th Squadron's B-26s, six were committed to the provision of air cover for the Norwegian freighter *Reinholt* as it chugged its way from Inch'ŏn to Fukuoka, Japan, with 682 Western refugees from Seoul on board. The remaining four B-26 light bombers, tasked to attack a tank column north of Seoul, were hampered by fading light and low cloud obscuring the ground.

Under extreme pressure from MacArthur to immediately fly the flag, Chief of Staff General Edward Almond called General Partridge to stress the need for 'visible supporting actions', adding that he wanted 'bombs on the ground in the narrow corridor between the 38th parallel and Seoul, employing any means and without any accuracy.'

A USAF
B-26-delivered
parachute demolition
bomb explodes
dramatically on a
North Korean target.
(Photo USAF)

U.S. FORCES TO STAY IN JAPAN

Quitting Reports Denied
American occupation forces are not to be withdrawn from Japan. Washington
made this clear yesterday in an official denial – the second in 24 hours – that such a
move was contemplated by the U.S.

Complicating the issue was the fact that whereas Tokyo dispatches did not
disclose the source of the official who is alleged to have made the statement about
a withdrawal, Mr Draper, in Washington, made his denial on behalf of Army
Secretary Kenneth Royall, who has been touring the Far East, including Japan.

It was believed throughout Washington that the high American official referred
to in Tokyo messages was in fact Mr Royall, now in Hawaii on his way back to
Washington.

The unnamed high American official was alleged to have said that America
might abandon Japan in the face of a war threat.

Mr Royall is expected to hold a Press conference immediately after his return to
Washington, where he is expected tomorrow, and then he will have an opportunity
to explain. – Reuter.

The Western Daily Press, Monday, 14 February 1949

While elements of the US and British navies were launching carrier-borne attacks against the invading KPA on the east coast, Washington ordered a naval blockade south of 41°N on the east coast, and south of 39° 30´N on the west.

From when North Korean forces crossed the 38th Parallel on 25 June 1950, it took only three days for the South Korean capital, Seoul, to fall. Seen by the KPA as a strategic and psychological target, the KPA 1st and 6th divisions were deployed to the right to secure the Kaesong–Munsan–Seoul axis to isolate elements of the ROKA north of the Han River near Seoul, and to move on the capital. In the centre, the KPA 4th Division would make their way down the Tongduch'ŏn–Ŭijŏngbu–Seoul corridor, while to their left, the KPA 3rd Division were to complete the envelopment along the Poch'ŏn–Ŭijŏngbu–Seoul line.

The ROKA 1st and 7th divisions, and elements of the Capital Division were to the north of Seoul, where they met the full force of the North Korean invasion on the first day. Meanwhile the ROKA 2nd, 3rd and 5th divisions moved north of the Han River from their initial position to the rear as reserves. On the 27th, these units engaged the North Koreans. By the following day, the capital was effectively under siege, as thousands of Korean refugees clogged the roads leading south out of the city – ROKA troops and government officials lost themselves in the civilian flood. The vast majority crossed the 1,000-yard-wide Han River by one of the four rail and road bridges that straddled it.

In the middle of the pitiful exodus ROKA chief of staff, General Ch'ae Pyŏng-dŏk, prematurely blew all four bridges at 1.30 a.m. on the night of the 27th. The plan had been to

Large tracts of the South Korean capital, Seoul, sustained considerable damage, 1950. (Photo ROK government)

destroy the one three-lane highway and three rail bridges only once KPA tanks arrived in Seoul. On one bridge alone 500–800 people were killed or drowned when the explosives on their bridge detonated. Of greater consequence was the fact that the general's act had sealed the fate of 44,000 ROKA troops on the northern bank. Arms and heavy equipment were all abandoned as the soldiers did whatever they could to escape certain death at the hands of the heavily indoctrinated North Koreans. ROKA's chief engineer became Ch'ae's scapegoat for the enormous blunder. He was executed almost immediately.

The most tragic casualty of conflict: a small South Korean child sits alone in the street, crying, after the fighting had passed through her village. (Photo US NARA)

That same night, the KPA 3rd Division entered Seoul. And it was at this time that Major General Church arrived at Suwŏn on his fact-finding mission for MacArthur. The rest of the city was captured on the 28th, and the North Koreans immediately set about rounding up South Korean soldiers, police officers and government officials to be shot.

The KPA 3rd and 4th divisions sustained 1,500 casualties, but the number of casualties suffered by the broken ROKA was impossible to assess. By nightfall of the 27th, only 6,000 had managed to cross the river to the south bank. Of the ROKA strength of 98,000 at the time of the invasion three days earlier, by the 28th, only 22,000 could be accounted for on the rolls.

The US Far East Air Force (FEAF), under the command of the United Nations Commission (UNC), commenced bombing sorties over the Kimp'o, Pyŏnggang, Yonpo and Wŏnsan airfields, the marshalling yards at Ŭijŏngbu, and selected bridges over the Han River.

On the morning of 28 June, in the 'foulest imaginable' weather, Lieutenant Bryce Poe II took off from Itazuke in an RF-80A jet aircraft to conduct a photographic reconnaissance of the designated target area north of Seoul. The first reconnaissance mission of the Korean War and the first US combat jet aircraft reconnaissance ever, Poe returned sanguine about conditions over the target area. Assuming that pilots could safely navigate the low-lying clouds over Kyūshū when taking off and landing, then combat sorties would be possible.

At 7.30 a.m., a strike force of twelve B-26s, 'The Reds', of the 3rd Bombardment Group, dropped parachute bombs on the marshalling yards at Munsan, just south of the 38th and less than twenty-five miles from Seoul. As they turned back at low level in a

USAF B-26 light bombers release quarter-ton demolition bombs in a raid over North Korea. (Photo US NARA)

southerly direction, the crews strafed and rocketed targets of opportunity along the railway and the main roads. This high-risk tactic proved expensive as the bombers attracted heavy ground fire. One B-26 lost an engine and was forced to go down at Suwŏn, while a second, riddled with gunfire, limped back to Ashiya where it was written off. The crew of a third lost sight of the Ayisha airfield in thick, low cloud, resulting in their B-26 crashing. There were no survivors. Later that day, a second wave of B-26 Invaders took off on the same mission, and although three of the bombers experienced mechanical problems that forced them to turn back, the rest went on to attack rail and road targets north of the capital.

For the F-80 jet interceptors, the risks were greater. Limited visibility and the 200-foot cloud ceiling made for hazardous operational conditions. At 310 miles from Itazuke, F-80 missions to the Han River stretched fuel limitations and left no margin for error. Aircraft fuel gauges were in the red as pilots returned to base, and if the weather did not permit immediate touch-down, then the pilot was left with no other option but to bail out to save himself. Despite this, Price persisted with his precious Shooting Stars, dispatching six flights of four each that afternoon. For the American pilots, the area just to the north of Seoul provided rich pickings: T-34 tanks, artillery, soldiers and vehicles. During the day, F-82 Twin Mustangs conducted eleven missions over Korea, mainly as top cover for the transports flying into Suwŏn.

Also on the afternoon of the 28th, the first US Boeing B-29 'Superfortress' heavy bombers were deployed. Four B-29s of the 19th Bombardment Group, armed with demolition bombs, split into two as they reached the operational area, to bomb, in pairs the parallel road and rail routes that ran from Seoul to Kapyong and from Seoul to Ŭijŏngbu. As part of MacArthur's show of strength, the aircrews were also instructed to bomb anything that they felt was warranted.

With the fall of the capital, the top priority had to be to stem the North Koreans at the Han River on the city's southern outskirts. More so than anyone else, General Church at the front was keenly aware of the implications should the North Koreans not be halted at the Han.

A B-29 of the US 19th Bombardment Group bombing a target in Korea. (Photo USAF)

At around 3 a.m. on 29 June, Church woke up fellow survey mission officer, USAF Lieutenant Colonel John McGinn, with an urgent request for the rail bridge across the Han that the retreating ROKA had failed to demolish to be bombed, together with the large build-up of KPA troops and armour on the north bank. It was too late, however, McGinn responded, to divert the B-29s that had already left their base at Kadena, Okinawa, on a mission to strike Kimp'o to the north of Seoul.

At 8 a.m., nine B-29s from 19th Group dropped their 500lb bombs across Kimp'o from only 3,000 feet. At the same time, two B-29s from the formation bombed Seoul's railway station. Over Kimp'o, three KPAF fighters – two Yaks and an unidentified aircraft – took on the American bombers, but the B-29 gunners shot down one of the Yaks, while badly damaging the unknown fighter.

In his daily situation statement on the 29th, General Stratemeyer committed Douglas B-26 Invader light bombers in support of ROKA troops on the ground. Concentrating on what remained of the Han bridges, the Invaders hit the middle bridge of the three rail structures spanning the river, taking care of the fresh floor being laid by the North Koreans. In addition to this, the Fifth Air Force executed twenty-two missions on the 29th in support of the South Koreans. In the morning, 8th Wing's Lieutenant Moran, following orders, flew his F-82 into Suwŏn to obtain from Church an overlay of mapped dispositions of opposing forces around Seoul. Armed with this critical intelligence, Moran returned to Itazuke where the fresh information proved invaluable to F-82 fighters flying in support of ground troops. Elements of the 68th Squadron became the first to use napalm bombs in the conflict, by jettisoning fuel drop-tanks as incendiary bombs.

As the day dragged on, specialized F-80 fighters from the 8th Fighter-Bomber Wing maintained an orbital patrol over the Han at 10,000 feet. The fighters were fully loaded

West of the Naktong River, near Waegwan, where USAF B-29s made a mass strike in August 1950. (Photo USAF)

with .50 cal. ammunition, forsaking external bombs and rockets for optimum machine-gun firepower. If, after fifteen to twenty minutes no hostile aircraft had appeared in the combat zone, the F-80s would return to Itazuke after strafing enemy road traffic in and around Seoul.

At the same time, to the south KPAF conducted six sorties against the airfield at Suwŏn, including one comprising six Yaks. During the morning, USAF F-80 jet fighters brought down two Soviet-made KPAF aircraft over Suwŏn: a Lavochkin La-7 fighter and an Ilyushin Il-10 ground-attack aircraft. Seizing a window of opportunity when, for a short while, US aircraft were absent over the airfield, the KPAF hit and totally wrecked a C-54 transport on the ground.

Up until now, Stratemeyer had felt hamstrung by strict restrictions that prevented him from neutralizing the KPAF and gaining US air superiority. The North Koreans operated from their own safe bases, to where they would retire when the skies over Seoul and Suwŏn became too hostile. With an unfettered, growing air threat from the north, MacArthur flew into Suwŏn in his personal C-54, *Bataan*. Under a heavy F-80 and F-51 'Mustang' escort, MacArthur arrived at Suwŏn where he met with Church and McGinn and other members of their staff to discuss the desperate situation. During their conference in

General Douglas MacArthur, Commanding General UN forces, inspects a disabled North Korean tank. (Photo US Defense Department)

the local school building, four KPAF Yaks arrived over the airfield. The meeting unceremoniously dashed outside to see a dramatic dogfight develop as the Mustangs tackled the enemy. While the Yaks were more manoeuvrable, they lacked the speed of the American fighters. On the ground, MacArthur and other spectators watched as the Mustangs shot down all four Yaks, with 80th Squadron's Lieutenant Orrin R. Fox notching up two kills.

Later quoted as having stated, 'North Korea air, operating from nearby bases, has been savage in its attacks in the Suwŏn area,' MacArthur verbally authorized Stratemeyer to cross the 38th Parallel to attack North Korean airfields.

The 8th Tactical Reconnaissance Squadron immediately capitalized on the new freedom by conducting photo-reconnaissance sorties over KPAF airfields north of the 38th. This mission facilitated the rapid – many argued overdue – deployment at 4.15 p.m. of eighteen B-26s from the 3rd Bombardment Group, their target the principal KPAF air base at the DPRK capital, P'yŏngyang.

The light bombers arrived over an unsuspecting P'yŏngyang as the sun was setting on the 29th, the first to conduct an air assault on North Korea. Fragmentation bombs dropped on hangars, revetments and aprons. A Yak-3 gallantly tried to defend the base, but his challenge was ephemeral, shot down by a B-26 gunner. An estimated twenty-five North Korean aircraft on the ground were rendered useless.

That evening in Tokyo planning for the following day's missions was already at an advanced stage. While the Fifth Air Force would continue in its ROKA support role, B-29s of the US Twentieth Air Force were being armed with 260lb fragmentation bombs for a mission against the KPAF air base at Wonsan, 120 miles northeast of Seoul on the North Korean east coast. Around midnight, Church put in another urgent appeal to Tokyo for

KOREAN WOMEN AND THEIR CLOTHES

A street full of Koreans suggests the orthodox notion of the resurrection. Everybody is in white robes, and even though a man has got only one suit in the world, it is clean. When he goes home at night, if he belongs to this poor class, he retires to bed and his wife washes and pummels his clothes. I say 'pummels', for ironing is an unknown art in Korea. After being washed the calico is stretched on a wooden block and then with a flat block of wood in each hand the woman pounds it for hours.

After sunset all Seoul rings with the dactylic tap-tap-tap, tap-tap-tap of these domestic voices of the night as with the incessant cry of a million strident insects. The dress of the women is extraordinary, and certainly to quote Dr. Johnson, they must have been at infinite pains to invent it, for by nature no one could be such a fool. The upper garment consists of sleeves and an apology for the body of a jacket about six inches deep and reaching therefore about three inches below the armpits. The skirt is a great big petticoat attached to a broad waistband which begins about six inches below where the jacket ends. Between the two there is nothing – nothing, that is to say, except six inches of dirty brown skin, exposing just those parts of the body which all other women in the world prefer to conceal. The effect is disgusting.

The Korean men, on the other hand, are fine fellows, tall, well-built, graceful, dignified, generally possessing regular features. They all have, too, a well-fed look, although the standard of physical living is about as low as is possible. Poverty reigns in Seoul – extreme, universal and hopeless.

Pall Mall Gazette, Monday, 11 March 1889

A USAF B-29 Superfortress undergoing essential maintenance at Kadena Air Base, Okinawa. (Photo USAF)

the remaining Han River bridges and massed North Korean troops to be bombed. For this, the 19th Group, which had just completed a long-distance change of station and were thin on the ground, required six hours to rearm the Superfortresses with demolition bombs. There was adequate time to redesignate the heavy bombers' mission targets and reroute them to Seoul instead, but the unavoidable delay that the change of ordnance would require would be counter-productive. The fragmentation bombs would remain in the B-29 bays, and aircrews instructed to hit North Korean troop concentrations and landing craft on the north bank of the Han.

The 30th saw a near total concentration of FEAF's air support aimed at enemy movements on the north bank, wherever they were spotted. At timed intervals, flights of fifteen B-29s bombed the east–west axis of the Han River, but results were inconclusive, with members of Church's staff reporting that strikes were too far from the river to have had any meaningful effect.

The heavy-bomber effort was followed with eighteen sorties by B-26s of the 3rd Bombardment Group, strafing, bombing and rocketing any North Korean movements they encountered. An earlier 13th Squadron flight had observed a massive crush of North

The light anti-aircraft cruiser USS *Juneau* (CLAA-119). (Photo US Navy)

Korean tanks, vehicles and troops waiting at the rail bridge bottleneck as their engineers relaid the wooden floor. According to the B-26 pilots, it was like a turkey shoot.

On 29 June, FEAF, employing 350 aircraft, flew 172 missions while on the east coast the USS *Juneau* bombarded North Korean ports.

At Suwŏn, a frustrated McGinn found, with limited resources, that he was unable to optimize on-target direction for incoming sorties. He possessed the same small-scale Korean maps that the pilots operating out of both Itazuke and Ashiya airfields were using, making it extremely difficult to accurately pinpoint targets in the fluid situation. Working almost entirely on his own, a lack of adequate communications compounded his inability to provide meaningful support targets. As a consequence, on the 29th, when ROK defences were threatening to collapse under North Korean pressure, McGinn could only facilitate twenty-five missions. Belatedly, FEAF instructed the Fifth Air Force to set up a tactical air-direction centre in Korea, preferably at Suwŏn, to coordinate air-support operations from close to the front. But it was too little, too late.

Should the US have exploited their air superiority to halt the invasion?

Purely from a tactical point of view, the North Koreans' apparent ignorance of the vulnerability of their long military columns from air attack was a major weakness that the

Railway bridges across the Kŭm River ten miles north of Taejon take direct hits from US bombers. (Photo US NARA)

Pakch'ŏn railway bridges being bombed by USAF B-29s, July 1950. (Photo USAF)

Americans could have used in their favour. It was also by now abundantly clear that there was little on the ground that could effectively – and literally – stop the KPA's armour in its tracks. Thirdly, the North Korean ground troops, perhaps naïvely, did not feel threatened by enemy aircraft – they had certainly not been trained in what evasive action to take in the event of attacks from the air. Commander of the US 49th Fighter-Bomber Group, Colonel Stanton T. Smith, said:

> In the early parts of the combat, the enemy troops were not too well indoctrinated in what airpower could do. Either that or they had a lot of guts, because we would time and time again find convoys of trucks that were bumper to bumper against a bridge that had been knocked out, and we'd go in to strafe them, and every man in the truck would stand up where he was and start firing his rifle at us. I don't think I would have done that with the power that we were putting down on them.

In the first few days in July, the Fifth Air Force used Japan-based B-26s, F-80s and F-82s in low-level attacks on KPA elements on the ground. Flying out of Iwakuni, most of the B-26s were B model, 'hard-nose' variants, armed with fourteen forward-firing machine guns, ideal for strafing ground targets. F-82s provided bomber escorts into North Korea, as well as striking targets along the Han River. F-80C jet fighters, based and drawn from the 8th, 35th and 49th fighter-bomber groups at Ashiya and Itazuke, flew regular daytime missions over Korea. Required to liaise with the army and air force in the operational areas for target allocation, the quick-changing situation on the ground made it difficult to safely identify enemy targets, unless there were robust and accurate ground-to-air directional communications.

By mid-July, 70 per cent of the missions conducted over Korea were by F-80s, accounting for 85 per cent of North Korean losses through air strikes. From 7 to 9 July alone, the Fifth Air Force claimed 197 KPA trucks and forty-four tanks on the Seoul–P'yŏngt'aek road. At this stage in its history, the F-80C lacked bomb pylons on the wings, but six .50 cal. nose guns more than compensated for its effectiveness at accurately strafing ground targets. The relatively new 5 in. high-velocity aircraft rocket (HVAR) 'Holy Moses' was the jet's only tank killer, but the American pilots had to learn to use the weapon while in actual combat. The best results were achieved at 1,500 feet and firing all four rockets at a 30° angle.

At the Han River, ROKA resistance was disintegrating at a catastrophic rate. While the main KPA thrust was aimed at Yŏngdŭngp'o industrial zone on the south bank, North Korean troops and armour were being ferried across the river, initially southeast of Seoul. Late on the afternoon of 30 June, the decision was made for the Advance Command in Korea (ADCOM) to immediately abandon Suwŏn. All encrypted material was burned before all personnel congregated at the airfield. At 9.40 p.m., General Church and Ambassador Muccio also arrived. The reluctant Church directed that ADCOM should move south by

vehicle and re-establish a new command post at Taejŏn, seventy miles away in a straight line. Before departing, Colonel McGinn's last act was to drive a jeep along the runway to prevent two approaching C-47s from landing. With an anti-aircraft artillery in place as a rear guard, the small American convoy drove through the airfield gates, where a large throng of unidentifiable Koreans had gathered, into the dark, rain-drenched night to Taejŏn.

The North Koreans had no reason to tarry in Seoul – their ultimate goal was to push the

High-velocity aircraft rocket (HVAR) 'Holy Moses' (upper) rockets mounted on a US Navy Vought F4U-4B Corsair aboard the carrier USS *Philippine Sea*. (Photo US Navy)

Americans off the tip of the peninsula and into the sea. Early on 1 July, a solid mass of KPA troops surged across the Han by bridge and by boat and, it was rumoured, some even swam across.

At the end of June, the Fifth Air Force, in an operation code-named 'Bout-One', deployed ten war-fatigued North American F-51 Mustangs to Taegu Airfield, to establish a combined US-South Korean combat wing commanded by Major Dean E. Hess. However, the South Korean pilots were too inexperienced at operating the weighty Mustang, so all combat missions were flown by American pilots. While also performing sorties in the central and eastern areas, the Mustangs were most active in support of the struggling US 24th Infantry Division. Hess recalled that the requests for this support were random and on an 'on-demand' basis, with even General Walker driving out to the airfield from his Eighth Army command in Taegu to request airstrikes:

> I recall on one occasion, individuals came out from KMAG in the middle of the night, about three o'clock in the morning, and they requested an air strike verbally just by sticking their heads in the tent and requesting an air strike over a city at a certain time and then disappearing in the night.

This 'fighting-fire' tactic was of growing concern to senior FEAF commanders, who saw the North Korean threat as one that stretched from coast to coast. MacArthur, on the night of 9 July, when he received news that the 24th had been driven out of Ch'ŏnan, started to question his ability to hold on to South Korea. Accordingly, he messaged FEAF: 'It is desired that all FEAF combat capabilities be directed continuously, and to the exclusion of other targets, at the hostile columns and armor threatening the 24th Division'.

US 24th Infantry Division howitzer and crew in action, July 1950. (Photo US Army)

Straddling the main arterial route south of Seoul, the KPA 2nd, 3rd and 6th divisions pushed down the western Suwŏn–Ch'ŏnan–Taejŏn axis. On 2 July, the unstoppable North Koreans enveloped Suwŏn, neutralizing residual ROK forces and a small US contingent. Just before they arrived, Office of Special Investigation (OSI) agent Donal Nichols, together with a group of South Koreans, had risked going back to the airfield to completely destroy the few damaged aircraft that had been left behind.

At the time of his visit to Suwŏn on 29 June, in the afternoon MacArthur had driven a short distance north along the Seoul road to assess for himself how ROKA defences were holding up. Back in Tokyo, MacArthur compiled a lengthy report for the JCS, revealing that the ROKA was down to less than 25,000 combat-fit but confused and leaderless troops. Heavy equipment and essential supplies had been abandoned in the ignominious retreat. MacArthur recommended the urgent deployment to the Seoul–Suwŏn front of a regimental combat team (RCT) to shore up the defence line. Assuming that this could be achieved, MacArthur would then have bought sufficient time to move two infantry divisions across from Japan to launch a counter-offensive. The general was under no illusions: 'Unless provision is made for full utilization of Army-Navy-Air team in this shattered area, our mission will at best be needlessly costly in life, money, and prestige. At worst, it might even be doomed to failure'.

The Pentagon received his message at 3 a.m. on 30 June, where Chief of Staff General Joseph 'Lightning Joe' Lawton Collins established a conference link with the Far East Command to discuss MacArthur's recommendations. However, MacArthur challenged Collins's statement that President Truman would need time to consider the proposals in depth before making the required executive decision, the resultant delay negating any possible conclusive ground operations. It might already be too late to save the airhead at Suwŏn.

At this point, Collins left the communications room to apprise Army Secretary Frank Pace by telephone of the time-sensitive crisis at the Han River. Pace in turn called Truman to relay the message. The president immediately approved the recommendation for the deployment of an RCT, while giving an assurance that he would give his answer about the mobilization of US infantry divisions within hours.

With the presidential endorsement firmly in place, in Japan MacArthur ordered the US Eighth Army to move its 24th Infantry Division, commanded by Major General William F. Dean, from Kyushu to Pusan by sea and air. He instructed FEAF to get ready to move divisional headquarters, two rifle companies of the 1st Battalion, 21st Infantry Regiment and an artillery battery to either Suwŏn or Pusan. Commanded by battalion CO Lieutenant Colonel Charles 'Brad' Smith, this was the RCT that MacArthur had asked for. It was given the eponymous title 'Task Force Smith'.

Across the Pacific, at 9.30 a.m. on 30 June, Truman met with his army, navy and air secretaries and chiefs of staff at the White House. After deliberations lasting only half an hour, Truman authorized MacArthur to employ in Korea whatever American forces were available to him without compromising Japan's security. Chief of Naval Operations Admiral Forrest Sherman's request to impose a naval blockade on the DPRK was also

US troops firing a 75mm M20 recoilless rifle, 1950. (Photo US Army)

authorized by the president. The United States was now at war with the North Korean forces that had aggressively crossed the 38th Parallel.

On 1 July, six C-54 transports ferried Task Force Smith from Japan to Pusan, from where the unit was trained north to Taejon, arriving in the South Korean town the following morning. The force comprised half of battalion headquarters company, half of the signals platoon, and below-strength B and C rifle companies. There were four 75mm recoilless rifles with crews: two from D Company, 1st Battalion and two from M Company, 3rd Battalion. The 21st Regiment's heavy-mortar company supplied two 4.2in. mortars and a private for each, while Company B provided mortar-support teams of five to six men for each weapon. In addition to the standard M1 carbine infantry rifle, the troops were equipped with six 2.36in. 'bazooka' hand-held rocket launchers and four 60mm mortars.

Each soldier was issued with 120 rounds of .30cal. ammunition and two days' C rations. Standard US army issue from 1948 to 1951 was the C-2 ration pack, containing precooked meals that could be consumed either hot or cold, and toiletry and confectionary items and cigarettes. The task force comprised seventeen officers and 389 regular infantrymen. Most of the infantrymen were aged twenty and under, with only 16 per cent having any combat experience.

A US bazooka team during the battle for Osan, July 1950. (Photo US Army)

KOREA ACTION APPROVED AT WESTMINSTER

Only Atomic Bomb Prevents Attack
The House of Commons at Westminster last night approved without a division a motion by [prime minister] Mr. Attlee endorsing the Government's action on Korea.

Mr Churchill, pledging the Opposition's support for the Government's action, said he thought they should try to come to a settlement with Russia but on the basis of strength, not weakness. There could be no better prelude to discussions with the Soviet than a defeat of the Communists in Korea.

Saying that the forces required for the defence of South Korea – or even its recapture – would not make any decisive difference to the defence of Europe, Mr Churchill went on: 'The immunity of Europe from attack depends

94

overwhelmingly on the vastly superior stock pile of atomic bombs possessed by the U.S. That is the sole deterrent which exists.'

Mr Attlee opened the debate by moving the Government motion: 'That this house fully supports the action taken by H.M. Government in conformity with their obligations under the United Nations Charter, in helping to resist the unprovoked aggress against the Republic of Korea.

Mr Churchill said: 'It is my belief that the American superiority in atomic warfare is, for the time being, an effective deterrent against a general Communist onslaught.

'One thing is essential now, namely, that the step which the Communists have taken in Korea should not end in triumph. If that were to happen, a third war in conditions more deadly than now will exist ... would be forced upon us before long,'

Belfast News-Letter, Thursday, 6 July 1950

Commanded by Lieutenant Colonel Miller O. Perry, artillery support came from elements of the 52nd Field Artillery Battalion. With a strength of nine officers and 125 men, the unit was equipped with five 105mm howitzers – all of Battery A – and 75 vehicles. A small element from headquarters and service batteries completed the strength.

In pursuance of his task, Smith straight away set off on the road north to Seoul to identify a tactical position on the road at which he and his men could dig in to stall the enemy in a delaying action until the arrival of the two infantry divisions from Japan – the 24th and 25th. About eight miles from Suwŏn – fifty miles from the capital – Smith found a line of low hills rising 300 feet above the countryside. The position provided a commanding and unobstructed view along the road. In the rough terrain, with few roads, this would be the KPA's line of advance on Osan, three miles to the south of the hills. The position felt right for purpose.

A 105mm howitzer in action along the US 1st Cavalry Division line. (Photo US NARA)

On 4 July, Perry arrived at P'yŏngt'aek with his artillery support, and late that afternoon he and Smith went along the road to reconnoitre the position Smith had selected. As night fell, the force moved out, leaving behind one of the howitzers. One of the senior officers likened the troops to 'a bunch of boy scouts' about to challenge 'tried combat soldiers'. At 3 a.m., leaving the artillery 2,000 yards to their rear, the convoy arrived at the position where they expected to find South Korean troops waiting for them on top of a hill next to the road. The hill, however, was unoccupied, and the Americans, wearing ponchos to keep out the persistent rain, attempted to dig foxholes in the unforgiving rocky hill. Most only managed a 'scrape', into which they curled up in the rain and tried to sleep. The American defensive line was a mile wide, straddling the road to Osan, but with no protection on their flanks. By this time, volunteers from the artillery had joined the infantry with four teams of .50cal. M2HB Browning machine guns and four bazooka teams.

At the foot of the hill, signallers were busy laying a telephone line to one of the howitzers that had been brought up to 1,000 yards south of the hills. The gun would serve as an anti-tank weapon and to bombard the road. Next to the road, several truckloads of ammunition had been unloaded, but no one appeared responsible to ensure that the boxes were lugged to the top of the hill.

At first light – gloomy and wet – Smith ordered all heavy weapons to be registration-fired to calibrate distance. Just after 7 a.m., nervous anticipation rippled along the hilltops at the sight of a column of eight dark-green tanks steadily approaching across the open plain from the direction of Suwŏn: Soviet-made North Korean T-34/85 tanks from the 107th Tank Regiment, 105th Armoured Division. Many still contend that the medium

A .50 cal. machine-gun squad of E Company, 2nd Battalion, 7th Regiment, US 1st Cavalry Division, fires on North Korean patrols, Naktong River, August 1950. (Photo Sergeant Riley)

T-34's mobility, hull armour, firepower and robust features won the war on the Eastern Front for the Red Army in the Second World War.

An hour later, the artillery forward observation officer (FOO) responded to a request from B Company commander Captain Dashner and the rear howitzers opened fire on the advancing tanks, now only 2,000 yards from the infantry.

Although divesting some of the tanks of KPA troops riding on the outside, the high-explosive rounds had no effect on the tanks, which were also travelling with their turrets hatches shut. The howitzer battery quickly expended its six armour-piercing, high-explosive, anti-tank (HEAT) shells, but with the same useless outcome.

At 700 yards, Smith employed the 75mm recoilless rifles, but despite scoring several direct hits, the impenetrable tanks clanked noisily forward unhindered, while periodically stopping to open fire with their main 85mm guns and coaxial 7.62mm Degtyaryov machine guns.

As the tanks broke through the infantry line, a lone lieutenant, Ollie Connors, snatched up a 2.36in. bazooka and proceeded to launch at close range no fewer than twenty-two rockets at the passing tanks. By the end of the Second World War, the 2.36 inch had become almost totally ineffective against a tank's heavily armoured body, and unfortunately, five years after the end of the conflict, the larger more powerful 3.5in. rocket launcher had not yet reached MacArthur's Far East Army. Connors's first projectile exploded harmlessly against the hull of the leading tank, and without pause or falter, the machine continued south down the road toward the US artillery line.

A knocked-out Soviet-made North Korean T-34/85 tank. (Photo US NARA)

As the tanks neared the single howitzer, HEAT shells finally scored with damaging hits to two of the T-34s. From one disabled machine, a crew member appeared from the hatch, firing one of the ubiquitous Soviet PPSh-41 'burp guns' that had been given to the KPA by Moscow in massive numbers. Before being shot and killed, the North Korean shot an assistant Browning machine-gun operator, possibly the first American killed in action in the Korean War. For many years, the name of Private Kenneth R. Shadrick was given as the first such fatality, but this is now believed by many historians to be incorrect. Shadrick was killed the following day at Osan. A third tank, firing its main gun, silenced Lieutenant Philip Day's recoilless rifle section, leaving the officer with blood streaming from his ears, but alive. From the first engagement until 10.15 a.m., an estimated thirty-three KPA tanks had smashed their way through Smith's flimsy blocking position, resulting in his force sustaining twenty casualties.

Less than an hour later, in which time the Americans barely had sufficient time to consolidate and take stock in the continuing rain, another three T-34s appeared from the north. This time, however, the North Korean armour was vanguard to columns of infantry from the 16th and 18th regiments, 4th Division. As the column approached Smith's 400-yard front, the KPA troops spread out to the east and west of the road, intent on enveloping the American flanks.

Wounded US soldiers receiving medical treatment at a first-aid station, near the front lines. (Photo US Defense Department)

As the tanks reached the 1,000-yard mark, Smith opened fire with everything they had, raking the KPA infantry. The tanks, however, kept rolling forward. As the T-34s came within 300 yards, they enfiladed the US hilltop positions with cannon and machine-gun fire. Smith's casualties were now starting to mount and the Americans were down to their last twenty rounds of ammunition each. Smith had lost communication with his artillery, leaving him to assume that the batteries had been destroyed. His situation was now untenable.

Smith, in consolidating a circular defence perimeter on the only high ground available to the east of the road, instructed C Company commander and war veteran Captain Richard Dashner to move his 150-odd men across the road to the east, where they should dig in and establish the best possible fields of fire. Among boulders below, medics were frantically attending to the wounded without any emergency supplies of whole blood.

The North Korean infantry now employed artillery, mortars and small arms. Smith, aware that he was about to be overwhelmed by the unstoppable North Koreans, ordered a withdrawal at 4.30 p.m. In the disarray, three of Smith's platoon commanders did not receive the order, and it was at this juncture that the Americans suffered their highest number of casualties.

It was evident, though, that there was no orderly withdrawal plan. Under heavy enemy fire, amorphous groups of C Company took to the paddy fields on either side of the road, teetering on the narrow embankments that interlaced the flooded rice fields. Weapons, equipment and anything else that would encumber a swift escape from the North Koreans were abandoned in the rout. Donald Knox, in his *The Korean War, an Oral History: Pusan to Chosin* (Harcourt Brace Jovanovich, 1985), quotes battalion officer Lieutenant Philip Day:

It was every man for himself. When we moved out, we began taking more casualties ... guys fell around me. Mortar rounds hit here and there. One of my guys got it in the middle. My platoon sergeant, Harvey Vann, ran over to him. I followed.

'No way he's gonna live, Lieutenant.'

Oh Jesus, the guy was moaning and groaning. There wasn't much I could do but pat him on the head and say, 'Hang in there.'

Another of the platoon sergeants got it in the throat. He began spitting blood ... For the rest of the day he held his throat together with his hands. He survived, too.

US Marines overlooking the Naktong River, August 1950. (Photo US Navy)

After ordering the withdrawal, Smith went searching for Perry, whom he found still in his original position to the east of the road, his artillery intact – only Perry and another soldier had been wounded. Making the five howitzers unusable by removing the breech-blocks and sights, the group of men headed into Osan, only to find KPA T-34s on the southern outskirts of the town. Forced to circumnavigate the now North Korean-held Osan, the Americans drove south to Ch'ŏnan.

INFANTRY IS STILL 'QUEEN OF BATTLE'

By our Military Correspondent
Lessons of the Korean battle front – first major test of war since 1945 – should come as a salutary reminder to the armchair strategists that there is still no push-button answer to battle.

After nine days' confusion, with their quota of flap and counter-flap, the following facts are beginning to emerge:

1. The infantryman still holds the key to success in battle;
2. Air (and naval) support purely from a tactical point of view can alone have no decisive effect on the war;
3. The most enthusiastic and patriotic troops are no match for a prepared and well-trained enemy.

Lack of armour has been blamed for the South Koreans' early setbacks – but how different the story might have been had there been first-rate infantry troops with even limited supporting weapons on the spot.

South Korea, with poor roads, paddy fields and broken country is not good terrain for armoured operations and there is no evidence that the Communists have made any bold use of their 33-ton Russian tanks.

Yet how quickly the word came back and with what speed were headquarters moved, when it was shouted that tanks were on the road! The point about that, I think, is that first-rate infantry being the most exposed of all troops in defence can either steady the whole army or render it liable to sudden panics, flaps and evacuations.

Let us consider the development of the battle from the active entry of United States forces. When the Superfortresses (strangely out of their role as strategic bombers), Shooting Stars and Mustangs roared overhead, the push-button enthusiasts might have been forgiven for leaning back to anticipate an early rout.

But what happened? Instead of presenting targets for the rocket-firing jets the miserable Communists regrouped their tanks by night, struck swiftly and then disappeared under cover again.

Yorkshire Evening Post, Tuesday, 4 July 1950

A wounded South Korean soldier is carried to a first-aid station by an American GI. (Photo US NARA)

After two harrowing days of forced marching, Dashner arrived at Ch'ŏnan, but with fewer than half of his own C Company. For B Company, however, it was far worse. Platoon commander Lieutenant Carl Bernard, his hands and face peppered with grenade shrapnel, had suddenly found his platoon, or what was left of it, alone on their hilltop position. At the base of the hill, Bernard discovered several medics trying to save the wounded.

Taking those wounded who could still walk, he split his platoon and the wounded in two before they went off separately. The more seriously wounded would have to become prisoners of war.

Another medic, Ezra Burke, also left the hill, together with his team of four medics, two stretcher cases and a walking wounded. Late that afternoon, dogged by advancing KPA troops all the way, Burke split the group, electing to go southwest and leaving the other group to decide on their best course of action. After a miserable and uncertain night and not knowing where they were, as dawn broke the following morning, the second group set off in a southerly direction. A while later they stumbled into Lieutenant Bernard with his group of seven men by a hill overlooking P'yŏngt'aek. Mentally and physically exhausted, the starving group of soldiers laid up during daylight hours, and moved at night. At great risk they entered villages to barter whatever they had on them for a bit of food.

On 10 July, five days after the one-sided battle at Osan, the pitiful group staggered into Taejon on swollen feet. Burke was airlifted to Japan the next day suffering from a painful kidney stone, while Bernard was operated on to remove the grenade fragments from his body.

At Ch'ŏnan, only 185 members of the battalion mustered after the Osan débâcle, which meant that 150 had been killed, wounded or were still missing. The KPA casualties were estimated at 42 killed and 85 wounded. They had lost four tanks, with a further three sustaining relatively minor damage.

Over the ensuing days, small groups or individual survivors of Osan trickled in to safety at various places. One infantryman, Sergeant William F. Smith, arrived in Pusan two weeks later, having hitched a ride on a boat along the west coast.

On 10 July, all available F-51s, B-26s, F-82s and F-80s were thrown at the KPA 3rd Division threatening the 24th Division. The combined air attack accounted for 117 trucks, thirty-eight tanks and seven half-tracks. Ten B-29 Superfortresses supported the mission by bombing KPA targets of opportunity on the road between Ch'ŏnan and Suwŏn. The Fifth Air Force executed 280 combat sorties on the day, but the North Korean war machine barely paused to recuperate before continuing the drive south.

The wisdom of America's precipitate entry in the war, largely fuelled by an impulsive MacArthur, will always come under critical scrutiny. To send a tiny, disjointed, ill-prepared and poorly equipped 'task force' to dam the Red tsunami from above the 38th Parallel, was a totally ill-conceived and naïve blunder by the decision-makers in both Tokyo and Washington. For Smith and his gallant party of mainly inexperienced young men, it was a suicide mission, which, at best, merely slowed the North Korean advance by seven hours.

Kim Il-sung's army continued on its southward blitzkrieg, ploughing through the 34th Regiment's 'blocking position' at P'yŏngt'aek on 6 July.

Just on 2,000 troops of the 34th Infantry Regiment had been moving up behind Smith's battalion, following Dean's orders to stall the North Koreans on the key southward routes at Ansong and P'yŏngt'aek. However, just as was the case with Smith, the 34th had no armour and no effective anti-tank weapons. Late at night on the 5th, they encountered the

Captured Soviet equipment, Naktong River. (Photo Corporal Laitinen)

first trickle of survivors from Osan. Numb with shock and almost incoherent, they spoke to their comrades about the tragedy that had befallen them just hours earlier.

In rain and dawn mist, against a greying sky, the 1st Battalion of the 34th (1/34th) suddenly found itself facing the North Korean juggernaut crossing a shallow stream into their position. What ensued was more ignominious than that of Smith's collapse at Osan. The Americans' machine guns and mortars did not even make the KPA armour flinch. Fearing envelopment, battalion commander Lieutenant Colonel Harold 'Red' Ayres, believing he had run out of options, ordered a retreat, but rout would be a better way to describe the Americans' abandonment of equipment and disorderly rush southward, lost in rivers of screaming refugees, their carts and their livestock. After only five hours, Ayres lost eighteen troops wounded and thirty-three missing to Major General Lee Kwon Mu's KPA 4th Infantry Division.

Upon hearing of yet another embarrassing defeat, General Dean raced up the Ch'ŏnan road to restore order and turn his men about to face the enemy. Finding his troops in full retreat, the stress of the moment boiled over into anger as Dean remonstrated with the 34th's senior officers, demanding that they dig in and hold their position. Without hesitation, Dean removed the regiment's commander from his position, replacing him with a unit officer who had Second World War combat experience. There would be more such

USAF F-80s strike North Korean marshalling yards. (Photo USAF)

field dismissals in those early weeks, as the Americans, largely lacking both mettle and the hardware, failed to even make a dent in the North Korean fighting machine.

On 6 July, while the North Koreans paused to consolidate and to allow logistical support from the north to strengthen, the last of the 24th Infantry Division troops arrived in Korea. Two days earlier, the 24th's commander, Major General William F. Dean had assumed command of the US Army Forces in Korea (USAFIK). The 51-year-old general had set up his headquarters, together with that of his division, at Taejŏn.

The role of the UN in the defence of the ROK was legalized on 7 July 1950 when the Security Council overwhelmingly approved Resolution 84. Pursuant to this document, on 10 July, US General Douglas MacArthur assumed command of the UNC.

Dean appointed Colonel Robert R. Martin to take over command of the 34th. Martin, a fellow officer of Dean's with whom he had served alongside during the Second World War, would be dead forty-eight hours later.

On the morning of 8 July, the KPA 16th and 18th infantry regiments, 4th Division, with T-34/85 tanks in support, clashed with the US 34th Regiment in Ch'ŏnan. The Americans were able to set one tank ablaze with five grenades, while disabling a further two with rocket launchers.

84 (1950). Resolution of 7 July 1950 [S/1588]

The Security Council,
Having determined that the armed attack upon the Republic of Korea by forces from North Korea constitutes a breach of the peace,
   Having recommended that Members of the United Nations furnish such assistance to the Republic of Korea as may be necessary to repel the armed attack and to restore international peace and security in the area,

1. *Welcomes* the prompt and vigorous supports which Governments and peoples of the United Nations have given to its resolutions 82 (1950) and 83 (1950) of 25 and 27 June to assist the Republic of Korea in defending itself against armed attack and thus to restore peace and security in the area;
2. *Notes* that Members of the United Nations have transmitted to the United Nations offers of assistance for the Republic of Korea;
3. *Recommends* that all Members providing military forces and other pursuant to the aforesaid Security Council resolutions make such forces and other assistance available to a unified command under the United States of America;
4. *Requests* the United States to designate the commander of such forces;
5. *Authorizes* the unified command at its discretion to use the United Nations flag in the course of operations against North Korean forces concurrently with the flags of the various nations participating;
6. *Requests* the United States to provide the Security Council with reports as appropriate on the course of action taken under the unified command.

Adopted at the 476th meeting by 7 votes to none, with 3 abstentions (Egypt, India, Yugoslavia).
   One member (Union of Soviet Socialist Republics) was absent.

Shortly afterward, Private First-Class Robert Harper, HQ Company, 34th, gave a first-hand account:

As daylight broke on July 8, we heard this loud clanking noise off on the left. We understood now what was happening – their tanks were coming. Eventually I could see them dimly, moving through the morning mist. I counted them. When I got to nine, an order was given to pull back off the railroad tracks and set up in the first row of houses behind the sewage ditch.
   From there I saw the North Korean infantry moving to my right across the field in front of the railroad depot. I could hear occasional small-arms and machine-gun fire. Mortar rounds began falling nearby. The tanks continued to roll down the road toward us. We had

no way of stopping them. They came to the end of the road and I could hear them firing. I did not know which of our companies were down there but knew they were catching hell.

We were ordered back to a narrow street, where we waited to see what would happen next. I heard the new CO, Colonel Martin, tried to take on one of the tanks with a bazooka. The tank scored a direct hit on the colonel, and he was killed on the spot.

We began receiving real heavy mortar and tank fire ... We ran down some alleys and met some more GIs who said orders had been issued to evacuate the town. I could hear a lot of small-arms and mortar fire behind me. We went to the east edge of town, worked our way through rice paddies and got to the road. We joined them in heading south. We drew heavy artillery fire and began to lose a lot of people.

Donald Knox, *The Korean War, an Oral History: Pusan to Chosin*

(Harcourt Brace Jovanovich, 1985)

On the 9th, in arguably the most chilling act of the young conflict, Lieutenant General Matthew Ridgway received a 'hot message' from MacArthur. The missive initiated a meeting of the JCS to weigh up the pros and cons of entrusting MacArthur with the employment of atom bombs against the North Koreans.

Chief of Operations, Lieutenant General Charles L. Bolté, was asked to speak to MacArthur on behalf of the JCS and to sound him out as to his tactical plans in which

Wearing peaked caps, General Douglas MacArthur (left), and commander of the First Marine Regiment, Colonel Lewis 'Chesty' Puller, Korea, 1950. (Photo USMC Archives)

atomic weapons would be his instrument of combat. Should ten to twenty atom bombs be made available to him, how would MacArthur propose to use them without 'unduly jeopardizing the general war plan'? MacArthur elaborated on his proposed tactical use of the weapons to capture Korea north of the 38th Parallel, and to employ against any Soviet or Chinese intervention:

> I would cut them off in North Korea. In Korea I visualize a cul-de-sac. The only passages leading from Manchuria and Vladivostok have many tunnels and bridges.
> I see here a unique use for the atomic bomb – to strike a blocking blow – which would require a six-months repair job. Sweeten up my B-29 force ...

However, in the absence of being able to predict the progress of the war with any degree of certain accuracy, the JCS determined that any use of atomic weapons at this early stage would be premature.

North of the 38th, with news streaming through of DPRK victories, the anti-American rhetoric in P'yŏngyang's press became overtly vitriolic, as in this July 1950 newspaper editorial:

> Look at Truman and the atomic warmongers – these bloodsuckers who want to suck the warm blood of our people and plunge our land into a sea of blood. What are they dreaming of and what are they after? It is very clear. They are dreaming of making a

B-29s of the US 98th Bombardment Group bombing targets in Korea. (Photo USAF)

colony of our beautiful fatherland and cheap slaves of the Korean people. They are after the fertile land which has been returned to the farmers who till it. They are after the gigantic factories which are being operated by the workers and all the democratic rights and freedoms which the workers are enjoying.

On 13 July, former XX Corps commander in General George S. Patton's US Third Army in the North-west Europe campaign of the Second World War, Lieutenant General Walton 'Johnnie Walker' Walker, established his Eighth Army headquarters in Korea. A veteran of both world wars, the short, stocky man from Texas was twice awarded the Distinguished Service Cross for extraordinary heroism, the Distinguished Service Medal for distinguished or meritorious service twice, the Silver Star for gallantry on three occasions, the Legion of Merit for exceptional meritorious conduct, the Distinguished Flying Cross for heroism in an aerial flight twice, the Bronze Star for heroic or meritorious achievement or service, and on twelve occasions, the Air Medal for meritorious achievement while participating in aerial flight.

A leader with such a pedigree in combat was needed to restore morale and turn the humiliating situation around. Syngman Rhee's army was close to total implosion, and the only close American reinforcements had to be drawn from occupied Japan, where the US 25th Infantry and 1st Cavalry divisions were being mobilized. From 10 to 15 July, the 25th Division arrived in Korea, followed on the 18th by the 1st Cavalry who landed at P'ohang on the east coast.

By 13 July, some 5,500 troops of Dean's battered 24th Division were in a defensive line on the Kŭm River, between KPA-held Ch'ŏnan and Taejŏn, site of US headquarters.

Troops of the 24th Infantry Regiment, US 25th Division, Korea. (Photo US NARA)

On a west–east axis, the 24th Reconnaissance Company held a five-mile section of the front, 3rd Battalion, 34th Infantry Regiment (3/34th) covered four miles, while the 19th Regiment, with fewer than 2,000 troops, was thinly spread out over a thirty-mile front. The 1/34th was held in reserve two miles back. The 21st Regiment, its combat-fit strength now significantly reduced to 1,100, was positioned near Taejŏn. That night, forty combat-fatigued troops, sole survivors of K Company, the 34th, were evacuated to the rear.

Later that evening, acting vice-commander of FEAF, Major General Laurence C. Craigie, met with General Emmett E. 'Rosie' O'Donnell, Jnr, at Far East Bomber Command headquarters to urgently draw up a plan to address the emergency crisis on the ground. Commander of the US Fifteenth Air Force, based at March Air Force Base, California, O'Donnell had established a temporary command in Japan when North Korea invaded the south. The following morning – 14 July – ten Superfortresses of the 92nd Bombardment Group took off from Yokota Air Base, Japan, in nine-minute intervals. Receiving instructions from 'Angelo' control at Taejŏn, the B-29s bombed targets at Chongju with moderate success.

At around 8 a.m., elements of the 16th Regiment, KPA 4th Division, started traversing the Kŭm to concentrate 500 troops two miles from the US 34th's left flank. Bombarding the Americans with heavy artillery and mortar fire, L Company was forced to pull back, while I Company on their right held firm until ordered at 9.30 a.m. to also withdraw. Both company commanders complained of not being able to communicate at all with battalion headquarters. Incredibly, they had not been made aware that their headquarters had in fact moved twenty miles south of the river to Nonsan, southwest of Taejŏn.

US Army personnel examine a Soviet 12.7mm (0.5in.) DshK 38-46 machine gun. (Photo US NARA)

Shortly before 2 p.m., the KPA overwhelmed the US 63rd Field Artillery Battalion, three miles south of the river. The 1/34th was then sent in to the abandoned position to rescue the wounded and to recover what equipment they were capable of moving. Despite having to face heavy incoming small-arms and machine-gun fire, the battalion was able to retrieve some of the vehicles and most of the wounded before retiring.

The 19th was ordered to hold their line as the 34th pulled back. On the extreme left of the flank, A, B and C companies of 1/19th were positioned along four miles of river front, with two platoons two miles to their left. Two miles to the right, E Company, 2/19th, defended a six-mile stretch. The rest of 2/19th was kept in reserve a mile to the rear. In support of the 19th, two miles to the rear of the regiment, the 13th and 52nd field artillery battalions (105mm howitzers) and the 11th Field Artillery Battalion (155mm howitzers) positioned their batteries.

On 15 July, elements of the KPA 3rd Division conducted a string of exploratory sorties, testing the strengths of the 19th's flanks while identifying gaps in their defences. At 3 a.m. on 16 July, the KPA struck en masse. The 19th's reserves launched a brave counter-attack, but in their attempt to take the battle to their assailants, the North Koreans circled in on their rear and blocked the road. As the hapless 19th were thrown back, they fell in to the waiting KPA roadblock, where they desperately fought to break through the enemy

US 27th Infantry Regiment, dug in near Pusan, 1950. (Photo US Army)

encirclement. The 19th suffered 650 casualties out of a strength of 3,400. Half of this number was from the 1st Battalion.

Having turned the Americans' flanks, the KPA drove Dean back into Taejŏn, where he immediately tasked the 34th Infantry Regiment commander, Colonel Charles E. Beauchamp, with organizing the town's defences. At 42, Beauchamp was the youngest regimental commander in Korea ... and the greenest. Having not seen any combat in the Second World War, in the post-war period he was, for various periods, posted to the staffs of the Infantry School, the Armed Forces Staff College, and the army's Counter-Intelligence School.

Fired up and eager to make his mark on the field of battle, Beauchamp also had at his disposal what was left of the 19th Regiment, the 24th Reconnaissance Company and the divisional artillery. In addition, Taejŏn was still base to a number of headquarters and service units.

To defend the western roads to Kongju and Nonsan, Beauchamp positioned the 1/34th and the 2/19th, to its left, on the Kapch'ŏn River. What few artillery pieces he had he moved from the Taejŏn airfield to the southern reaches of the town, while the 3/34th covered the north and west. Elements of the 21st Infantry Regiment, independent of Beauchamp's command had been deployed along a four-mile hilly front about four miles

US and South Korean forces, and civilians, evacuate Taejŏn. (Photo US NARA)

to the east of Taejŏn. Their principal objective was to keep the eastern route out of the town clear of the enemy.

On 18 July, Lieutenant General Walker arrived on a fleeting visit to tell Dean to hold Taejŏn for at least two days to allow him to deploy the US 1st Cavalry, fresh from Japan, on the road to the south.

Beauchamp would later record that Walker had in fact requested three days, adding:

> We could have withdrawn on the night of July 19/20 with probably no losses. I feel that to some extent I influenced General Dean to stay on the 20th. I felt very confident on the evening of July 19th that we could hold the enemy out of Taejon another day and believe I so told General Dean.

On 19 July, General O'Donnell of Bomber Command dispatched forty-seven B-29s from 19th and 22nd groups to bomb Seoul's rail marshalling yards, while eight B-29s from 92nd Group attacked tactical targets provided by Angelo. Part of this wing was also sent to the extreme left of the front line to bomb massing troops and tanks near Kongju. To the centre a misinterpretation of the target resulted in three B-29s bombing Andong, killing twenty-two civilians. On 17 July, B-29s destroyed two bridges and bombed rail marshalling yards at Chech'ŏn, Wŏnju and Hoengsŏn.

It soon became evident, however, that the strategic-bombing role of the B-29s could not be effectively converted to orally supplied tactical targets. Operating at 10,000 feet and with limited Angelo information, at best only approximate target areas could be bombed. Disagreeing with MacArthur's contention that the employment the B-29s in emergency procedures to tackle emergency situations was justified, FEAF commander General Stratemeyer was emphatic in his protestations that the use of Superfortresses as an emergency measure was wasteful in the extreme: 'You cannot operate B-29s like you operate a tactical air force. B-29 operations must be carefully planned in advance and thought out.' MacArthur relented, and on 18 July he issued Stratemeyer with written orders confining the employment of B-29s in the area between the 'bomb line' and the 38th Parallel. The objective would be to isolate the battlefield.

By this time, the Americans had also gained air superiority over the North Korean People's Air Force (KPAF). In the first fortnight of July, US aircraft came under constant harassment from KPAF Russian-made Yak fighters, bringing down a B-29 and damaging other aircraft. The North Korean fighters were dispersed widely across the peninsula, so MacArthur instructed Stratemeyer to divert part of his force to neutralize the KPAF wherever they were hiding. On 15 July, the airfield at Kimp'o was strafed, destroying three Yaks on the ground. On the same day, O'Donnell diverted three of his B-29s to render the runways at Kimp'o unusable. On the 18th, aircraft from Task Force 77 carriers struck at P'yŏngyang airfields, destroying fourteen and damaging thirteen KPAF aircraft camouflaged on the ground. On the eastern coastal belt, on the 19th, carrier-borne aircraft destroyed a total of eighteen KPAF aircraft at Yonpo and Sondok.

USAF B-29s on a bombing mission. (Photo USAF)

That afternoon, seven F-80s of 8th Fighter-Bomber Group, led by Lieutenant William T. Samways, flew a mission just to the north of the 38th Parallel. Photographic air reconnaissance had revealed the presence of twenty-five North Korean aircraft under tree branches near the North Korean town of Pyŏnggang. Strafing at low level, the F-80 pilots destroyed fourteen KPAF fighters and a lone twin-engine bomber. Buoyed by the success of the overall operation, on 20 July, Stratemeyer sent fourteen B-29s to crater runways at Heijo and Onjing-ni airfields in the Pyŏnggang area.

The Americans now had almost complete control of the skies over South Korea. However, intelligence pointed to the fact that the KPAF still possessed around thirty operational aircraft. Repair work had also been undertaken on the runways at Kimp'o and Suwŏn.

Before sunrise on 20 July, the KPA 5th Regiment launched an attack on the 1/34th. As the Americans fell back, they exposed the 2/19th's right flank, forcing it to also retire. Brushing aside a half-hearted counterattack by the 3/34th – whose commander had strangely gone missing – the North Koreans had cleared the road to Taejŏn by 10 a.m.

With the arrival of more effective 3.5in. rocket launchers, the American defenders neutralized eight T-34s as they entered Taejŏn. Dean personally led a team that accounted for one of the KPA's tanks, but this had taken him away from the central command post at a critical period of the battle. To compound the lack of senior decision-making, Beauchamp and his executive officer were also away from the now rudderless control hub. Confusion, hesitation and a marked lack of clear orders was the calamitous outcome.

The Americans had a near-impossible fight to get out of Taejŏn in which they were now entrapped, sustaining horrific casualties in the process. Beauchamp escaped later with a small group of men. At a bottleneck created by a road tunnel, the fleeing Americans put up minimal ambush-style resistance, but it was a futile attempt to salvage a now hopeless situation – yet another rout. In small groups, the American troops bombshelled cross-country, but many could not escape the Red net, either killed or wounded.

Just on 4,000 GIs had entered the battle to prevent Taejŏn from becoming another North Korean victim. The aftermath would reveal that more than 1,100 had become casualties.

Arguably, the greatest – and most embarrassing – loss, was that of Major General William Dean, commander of the US 24th Infantry Division, who had become separated from his men and captured by the KPA.

With a small force of the 34th, in his jeep Dean followed a convoy of fifty vehicles evacuating the last of the regiment from the town. By now, there was a profusion of KPA roadblocks on all of Taejŏn's arterial routes, and as the column ran in to one such position, Dean's driver took a wrong turn, separating the occupants from the rest of the force. They managed to evade several KPA roadblocks as they left the town, but were eventually forced to abandon their jeep to cross the Taejŏn River, from where they scaled a nearby mountain.

General Dean's kill! (Photo US NARA)

MISSING GENERAL

Seen Making for U.S. Lines
With U.S. Forces in Korea, Sunday. –

Major-General William Dean, commander of the U.S. 24th Division, officially listed last night as missing in action, is known to have escaped from Taejon.

An American subaltern, Lt. Arthur Clark, who reached the U.S. lines to-day after a two-day trek, reported he had met the general in the hills south of Taejon on Thursday. He told the lieutenant he would return.

Lt. Clark said that when he last saw General Dean he was leading 40 men through Communist-held territory to the American lines. They had arms of various types, and were heading downhill towards a river.

Announcing last night that General Dean had been officially listed as missing, General MacArthur said: 'High hopes exist that he will return with one of the groups of separated personnel frequently returning to their units. General Dean's interpreter, who had been with him, indicates that Dean was wounded.'

The Scotsman, Monday, 24 July 1950

At some stage during their difficult progress through the mountains, Dean suffered a bad fall, gashing his head and fracturing his shoulder, and knocking himself unconscious. When he came to, he found himself alone and in considerable pain.

Dean crisscrossed the mountains for the next thirty-six days, hungry and in unrelenting pain. On 25 August, two South Koreans, ostensibly leading him to safety, handed Dean over to KPA troops. After brief incarceration in a prison camp near Suwŏn, Dean was moved to a POW camp in Seoul with other American army captives. It was here that he was recognized for who he was, and immediately translocated to larger, underground quarters in P'yŏngyang. Though relatively well looked after compared to other POWs, Dean was kept isolated and rigorously interrogated, but never tortured. Dean refused to talk, and on a few occasions, tried unsuccessfully to escape. After the cessation of hostilities, the repatriation of POWs took place in Operation Big Switch. Dean was freed on 4 September 1953, and flown home to a hero's welcome, complete with several decorations, including the Medal of Honor, and a ticker-tape parade in New York.

On 22 July, with Dean still listed as missing, Major General Church was given the command of the US 24th Infantry Division.

By this time, the US 1st Cavalry and US 25th divisions had been deployed, allowing the decimated 24th Division to be withdrawn for a bit of respite. In just seventeen days, the division's strength had plummeted by 30 per cent, including 2,400 men listed as missing in action.

A US 1st Cavalry Division soldier at his post on the Naktong River, August 1950. (Photo US Army)

However, the baptism of fire for the fresh troops from Japan raised more than just the issue of the deployment of largely inexperienced troops into what was effectively a fighting retreat. On 20 July, after a brief engagement of a few hours with the KPA at Yechon, east of Taejŏn, troops of the US 25th Division's 24th Infantry Regiment fled the battlefield, a worrying pattern that persisted in the following days. First Lieutenant Jasper R. Johnson, commander of K Company, 3/24th, had entered the town that afternoon, but after discovering that the 3rd Battalion had failed to secure a ridge overlooking Yechon, requested and was granted permission to withdraw.

On 29 July, after enduring a sustained KPA mortar bombardment, incomprehensible panic spread through the 1/24th like wild fire. So great was the threat of this collapsing the American line, that roadblocks were erected to the south of the battalion to stem the flow of deserters from the front line.

The regiment consisted mainly of African Americans, with black and white officers, despite the desegregation in 1948 of the US military by President Truman's Executive Order 9981. From the end of the Second World War until early 1947, the 24th Regiment was garrisoned on Okinawa, before being moved to Japan as a regular unit of the 25th Infantry Division. Washington identified the urgent need for full integration of African Americans into white units, but Korea was neither the time nor the place.

Walker then realized that the 24th could only be used as a 'tripwire' to alert other regiments. To this end, a reserve regiment was permanently kept in place behind the front to plug the gap should the 24th break.

From 20 July, the KPA 15th Division and the US 25th Division clashed for eleven days in and around the village of Sangju, forty-five miles east of Taejŏn. Situated in the centre of South Korea, Sangju sat on the mountain-roads junction just south of the Mun'gyong Plateau. The dividing watershed between the Han and Naktong rivers, the commanding vista of the Naktong Valley made Sangju a desirable strategic objective. Among a constant southward stream of fleeing civilians and ROKA troops, there had been sporadic and isolated engagements on the Mun'gyong Plateau between the KPA and the retreating ROKA when the US 25th Division arrived.

At this time, division commander Major General William B. Kean's 13,000-strong command was dispatched by General Walker to strengthen the crumbling ROKA line along the mountain corridors. The North Koreans should not be allowed to enter the Naktong Valley.

At Yechon, mentioned a little earlier, there was confusion on the morning of 21 July when, after an artillery and mortar bombardment that had set the town ablaze, Colonel

General Douglas MacArthur inspects US24th Infantry at Kimp'o. (Photo US NARA)

Henry G. Fisher, CO of the US 35th Infantry Regiment, came across from Hamch'ang to find Yechon deserted. Encountering only light resistance, the 3/24th returned to occupy the town by 1 p.m., sustaining only fourteen casualties as they moved in. The battalion then handed the town over to the ROKA Capital Division, denying Yechon to the KPA 8th Division for the rest of the month.

Kean was now able to concentrate on the vital task of holding the Sangju area with his 25th Division. To achieve this he had to protect the two routes into Sangju. To the north, after traversing the plateau, the main road passed through the foothills hamlet of Hamch'ang, fifteen miles north of Sangju. The other was a secondary road dropping out of the mountains farther west, before turning east toward Sangju.

Kean deployed the 2/35th in a blocking position behind ROKA units to the northwest of Hamch'ang, supported by tanks from A Company, US 79th Heavy Tank Battalion (M24 Chaffee tanks) and A Battery, US 90th Field Artillery Battalion (105mm howitzers). The 1/35th was deployed to reinforce the US 27th Infantry Regiment on the next north–south line of communications (LOC) westward.

The 2/35's hilltop position was on the southern side of a tributary of the Naktong that flowed past Sangju. An ROKA battalion was positioned to the north of the rain-swollen stream. The 25th's assistant division commander, Brigadier General Vennard Wilson, ordered F Company of the 2/35th to the centre of the ROK line, a command that met with vociferous protests from the battalion CO, Lieutenant Colonel John L. Wilkins: placing green infantrymen in such a vulnerable front-line position was questionable. The colonel's overt misgivings would be vindicated.

On 22 July, the KPA struck at the South Koreans' position, causing them to retreat but without informing F Company that they were doing so. It transpired that the ROKA move had been pre-planned to enable a consolidation with US forces to the rear. Anticipating orders, F Company did not reposition themselves to protect their now exposed flanks. The KPA rapidly capitalized on the situation to attack the stranded Americans from the rear. Chaos ensued, as the overwhelmed men took off in all directions to avoid imminent death or capture. The flooded river was impassable and several drowned. As the wounded and desperate crowded on the northern bank, US tanks opened fire, holding off the enemy to allow most of them to cross to their own lines. F Company suffered terribly: six killed, ten wounded and a staggering twenty-one missing.

The following morning, five KPA T-34s crossed the stream, but the 90th Field Artillery howitzers immediately accounted for four, forcing the fifth to race back to the North Korean positions.

On 23 July, the 2/35th was ordered back to a position five miles north of Sangju. Five days later, they were compelled to relocate two miles farther south, and by the end of the month, they found themselves in a hilly blocking position on the Kimch'ŏn road, eight miles south of Sangju. The 35th had retired thirty miles in eleven days, not through pressure from the North Koreans but merely in compliance with divisional orders. The ROKA 6th Division, meanwhile, whilst putting up a good fight on the mountain road from Mun'gyong, were steadily being pushed south by the KPA 1st Division. On 24 July,

Private First Class Benjamin Livingston flies as a gunner on a B-29 of the US 98th Bombardment Group. (Photo US NARA)

the South Koreans knocked out seven North Korean T-34 tanks in the mountains over-looking Hamch'ang.

Three days later, after being relieved by the US 24th Infantry Regiment northwest of Sangju and moved to bolster the Hamch'ang front, the ROKA 1st Division destroyed another four enemy tanks and captured one intact. Upon being relieved by the US 27th Infantry Regiment on the Hwanggan–Poun road, the depleted ROKA 2nd Division was absorbed by the ROKA 1st Division, which now meant that the US 25th Division had replaced the South Koreans to the west on the Sangju–Taegu axis. The amalgamated ROKA 1st and 2nd divisions were then moved into the northeast quadrant beyond Sangju on the Hamch'ang front.

By 27 July, the KPA had taken the Mun'gyong divide and were penetrating the upper reaches of the Naktong Valley near Hamch'ang. Simultaneously, the inexperienced young troops of the KPA 15th Division attacked Sangju, while to the west more KPA units were advancing along the secondary road from the mountains.

During this period of a renewed southward thrust by the North Koreans, north of Hamch'ang F Company of the US 35th Regiment gave a good account of themselves against KPA forces which outnumbered them three to one, before executing an orderly withdrawal. The Americans had inflicted heavy casualties on the enemy.

Twenty miles northwest of Sangju, the US 2/24th and elements of the ROKA 17th Regiment clashed with the KPA 48th Regiment, vanguard of the 15th Division. While

KOREA: 'STAND FAST'

America's Eighth Army in Korea have been told 'to fight to the death without giving another inch of ground.'

Lieut.-General Walker, Commander of the United States ground forces, gave this order to-day after flying close to the front line.

Landing in a village street he told officers 'Surrender is impossible. We must hold on the line we now have. There will be no Dunkirk, nor is there going to be a Bataan.'

A United States Army spokesman estimated to-day that the North Koreans had lost 31,000 killed and wounded.

Despite official assurances that all was well on the south coast and inland, the Communists were still fanning out behind their slowly advancing spearheads. They are now through the mountains in two places.

The latest official announcement put them as far west as Ponggyeri, only 65 miles from the vital supply port of Pusan.

Portsmouth Evening News, Saturday, 29 July 1950

GIs compare the larger, more effective 3.5in. bazooka with the smaller 2.36in. bazooka. (Photo US Army)

E Company of the 2/24th led F Company through a narrow gorge, they came under mortar and rifle fire from above. Openly ignoring their officers' orders to stand and take on the enemy, the troops turned and stampeded back in complete disarray, discarding their weapons as they ran. Hearing of the chaotic retreat, regimental commander Colonel Horton V. White drove to the spot to restore order. His efforts, however, were in vain, as the soldiers had ceased to be a cohesive entity. The next day, the ROKA 17th Regiment successively surrounded and neutralized the North Korean position that had panicked the 24th's companies. The South Koreans continued to engage the enemy in limited combat in the mountains, until they were completely withdrawn for a re-organization of ROKA forces around Pusan. The US 24th Infantry Regiment was the only force left behind to protect Sangju's western approaches from the Mun'gyong Plateau.

By 26 July to the end of the month, the US 24th Infantry, supported by batteries from the 64th, 90th and 159th field artillery battalions, was slowly retiring back along the western route to Sangju, pushed by elements of the KPA 15th Division. Casualties were mounting on both sides, while the Americans' resupply became increasingly tenuous. A cycle of fighting the North Koreans by day then falling back under cover of darkness evolved.

On 29 July, heavy KPA mortar fire caused sixty casualties to the 1/24th, once more evoking seemingly uncontrollable fear among the troops. As the men prepared their defences for the night, anxiety again sparked endemic panic and the disorderly evacuation of the position ensued once more. All that was remaining on the front line that night were Colonel White, the 77th Combat Engineer Company and a battery of the 159th Field Artillery Battalion. In a repeat of previous such occurrences of mass desertion, nothing that the officers – including White – could say or do halted the exodus. Frantically defending their position, that night the artillery battery fired in excess of 3,000 rounds into the darkness to keep the North Koreans at bay.

In the battle's death throes as July drew to a close, regimental officer Major John R. Woolridge set up a roadblock on the western outskirts of the town where he stopped every American army vehicle to vet the occupants and prevent deserters from leaving. In this manner, Woolridge netted an average of seventy-five absconders a day, and 150 on the last day of the battle.

By 30 July, the regiment had imploded so badly, that General Kean was compelled to recall the 1/35th to execute a holding position to facilitate the withdrawal and consolidation of the 24th. The following day, the North Koreans continued to press the Americans' fragile line. At this point, First Lieutenant Leon A. Gilbert, the African-American commander of A Company, and fifteen of his men unilaterally left the line. After refusing orders to resume his position on the basis that he was scared, Gilbert was arrested, court martialled and sentenced to death. The sentence was later commuted to seventeen years in prison. Following a huge outcry and a powerful African-American lobby, Gilbert served only five.

On 31 July, the 1/35th covered the full withdrawal of American forces, leaving the KPA 15th to walk into Sangju the next day, while the Americans and Koreans made plans to defend Masan on the southern coast of the Korean peninsula.

Following the fall of Taejŏn on 21 July, retreating US forces established a blocking position north of the village of Hwanggan, and ten miles east of Yŏngdong. The North Koreans would have to pass through the village to hit the main Seoul–Pusan highway. This would place the KPA to the rear of the US 1st Cavalry Division, at the same time severing its main supply line from the south. Arriving on the night of 22/23 July, for nearly a week the US 27th 'Wolfhounds' Infantry Regiment, 25th Infantry Division, would stall the KPA 2nd Division's advance. The US 25th Infantry Division, however, had also paid the price of the major disciplinary issues in the 24th Infantry Division by losing some of its most experienced officers to that troubled unit. At the same time, the Americans also relieved the fatigued ROKA units at Hwanggan.

Regimental commander and former airborne commander, Colonel John H. 'Iron Mike' Michaelis immediately confirmed his reputation as an effective commander. With leadership skills honed in the Second World War Western Europe theatre, Michaelis was a disciple of unit integrity as the fundamental key to surviving enemy envelopment.

On the morning of 23 July, Lieutenant Colonel Gilbert J. Check moved the 1/27th Infantry northward toward Poun, with the specific objective of engaging the North Koreans. That evening, a battalion patrol ambushed a KPA column just north of Poun, causing the North Koreans to halt and wait for first light the next day to attack the American position. With a heavy mist shrouding Poun, the KPA were able to get very close to the 1/27th forward

F4U-4B Corsairs of US Fighter Squadron 54 prepare to take off from the aircraft carrier USS *Valley Forge*, 1950. (Photo US Navy)

position before being seen. As the neared the two battalion companies on low ridges on either side of the road, they initiated mortar fire on the Americans.

Now typical of the KPA advance down the peninsula, their T-34 tanks appeared next, splicing the 1/24th's forward positions and firing on the battalion's command post. On the right KPA troops overwhelmed the battalion observation post and B Company's outpost line.

At this time, another five T-34s appeared, making for the US 71st Tank Battalion. Facing a rapidly deteriorating situation, Check called in an air strike to take out the North Korean tanks. With the support of three F-80 Shooting Stars firing 5in. rockets, the Americans knocked out six of the KPA 2nd Division's eight tanks.

On the night of 24 July, concerned about enemy envelopment, the 1/27th was withdrawn to the rear of the 2/27th. Oblivious to this development, early the next morning the North Koreans deployed two battalions to encircle what they thought was still the 1/27th's position. Now exposed in the open, the KPA were subjected to heavy and sustained tank, artillery, mortar and small-arms fire from the Americans. Heavy casualties were suffered

US Marines at Pusan, August 1950. (Photo US Army)

by the enemy and thirty of their number were taken prisoner. Almost impossibly, however, the KPA 2nd Division persevered, forcing Michaelis to issue another withdrawal order at 10 p.m..

On 26 July, the 1st Battalion, US 35th Infantry Regiment (1/35th) arrived to augment the 27th Infantry's right flank. However, the regiment's left flank remained vulnerable, where there was a large gap between C Company of the 27th, and the US 7th Cavalry Regiment, the nearest elements of the US 1st Cavalry Division. As the battle continued unabated, C and B companies took heavy losses – the former suffered 40 per cent casualties.

Early on 28 July, the KPA breached the 1/27th's line, causing C Company to quickly withdraw in the face of overwhelming numbers of North Korean infantry swarming down on them.

To avoid a likely rout, Michaelis was left with only two options if he had any hope of saving his 27th Regiment: withdraw the 27th through the US 1st Cavalry Division, or seek immediate support from the cavalry division. After consulting with the cavalry division commander, Major General Hobart R. Gay at his Hwanggan headquarters, Gay communicated with Eighth Army command for a decision. Michaelis was ordered to withdraw.

Before first light on 29 July, Michaelis passed through the 1st Cavalry's line to take up a new position just to the east of Kimch'ŏn. Later that same day, Eighth Army issued fresh orders for Michaelis to move farther southeast to Waegwan on the Naktong River, close to Taegu. In the fighting on the Hwanggan road, the US 27th Infantry Regiment had suffered 323 combat casualties: fifty-three killed, 221 wounded and forty-nine missing in action. The KPA 2nd Division losses were estimated at 3,000, chiefly inflicted by US artillery and armour.

The US 1st Cavalry Division, initially preparing to fill the gap in the front line left by the withdrawal of the 27th, was then threatened by the KPA 3rd Division skirting their left flank and taking Kimch'ŏn, and in doing so, cutting off Gay's vital supply line to Pusan.

Consequently, on 31 July, the 1st Cavalry, having sustained 916 casualties at Hwanggan and Sangju, was moved to the Naktong River. By executing what may, in hindsight be regarded as rear-guard actions, the retreating US 1st Cavalry, 24th and 25th divisions, had bought the UN forces sufficient time to establish the defensive Pusan Perimeter. There had been, however, a substantial disparity in the comparable performances in combat of the three divisions.

As at the end of July 1950, US casualties in the Korean conflict stood at 1,059: ninety dead, 294 wounded and 595 missing.

In the second volume in this series on the Korean War, the author will look at the United Nations Command's desperate fight for survival in the Pusan Perimeter.

Scene of a massacre, the twin-underpass railroad bridge at No Gun Ri, South Korea, where U.S. forces slaughtered between 250 and 300 Korean refugees, mainly women and children, later in July 1950. (Photo No Gun Ri International Peace Foundation)

A depiction of the massacre under the No Gun Ri bridge from the 2009 South Korean feature film *A Little Pond*. (Photo Nogunri Production)

U.S. 1st Cavalry Division troops withdraw southward on 29 July 1950, the day a division battalion pulled back from No Gun Ri after killing large numbers of trapped South Korean refugees there. (Photo Sgt Marques / U.S. Department of the Army)

SELECTED BIBLIOGRAPHY

Clayton, Dr Laurie, Center for the Study of Intelligence, *The Korean War and the Central Intelligence Agency*

Futrell, Robert F., *The United States Air Force in Korea, 1950–1953* (Progressive Management, first published 1983)

Halliday, Jon & Cumings, Bruce, *Korea, the Unknown War* (Pantheon Books, New York, 1988)

Lee, Colonel Suk Bok, Republic of Korea Army, *The Impact of US Forces in Korea* (National University Press, Washington DC, 1987)

Military Intelligence Section, General Staff, United Nations Command, *Korea, A Summary 25 June 50–28 April 52* (16 December 1953)

Tucker, Spencer C. (ed.) *Encyclopedia of the Korean War, A Political, Social, and Military History* (Checkmark Books, New York, 2002)

US Central Intelligence Agency, various declassified reports on the Korean War.

ABOUT THE AUTHOR

Born in Southern Rhodesia, now Zimbabwe, historian and author Gerry van Tonder came to Britain in 1999. Specializing in military history, Gerry has authored *Rhodesian Combined Forces Roll of Honour 1966–1981*; *Book of Remembrance: Rhodesia Native Regiment and Rhodesian African Rifles*; *North of the Red Line* (on the South African border war), and the co-authored definitive *Rhodesia Regiment 1899–1981*. Gerry presented a copy of the latter to the regiment's former colonel-in-chief, Her Majesty the Queen. Gerry writes extensively for several Pen & Sword military history series including 'Cold War 1945–1991', 'Military Legacy' (focusing on the heritage of British cities), 'Echoes of the Blitz', 'Death Squads' (on massacres and genocides) and 'Architects of Terror'.